The Magic of Style

THE MAGIC OF STYLE

By Larisa Kronfeld

ISBN: 978-0-9963182-0-4

First Edition 2015

Printed in China by Shenzhen Caimei

through Four Colour Imports, Ltd., Louisville, Kentucky.

Attributions

Cover and Interior Design: T.L. Price Freelance

Illustrations: Rosemary Fanti • Photographers: Derek Katana, Katana Photo, Inc.

Krzysztoof Babiracki • Kasia Jarosz • Mila Samokhina

In-store Photos taken in the Yolanda Lorente Boutique, Chicago, Illinois

LARISA KRONFELD

The
Magic
of
Style

HOW TO USE CLOTHES
TO LOOK MORE ATTRACTIVE

Author's Note

Although written in a conversational style, the information presented in this book is by no means simple or trivial. I chose the informal, conversational style to make the book easier to comprehend and retain. This book is full of insightful, substantive observations and recommendations, and offers many "pearls of wisdom," guidelines, advice and important nuances — way too many to easily absorb and retain with a more formal writing style. In addition, many words, phrases and concepts are also purposely repeated in different parts of the book to help understanding and retention. So, please don't be fooled by the humorous, informal writing. I hope you enjoy reading *The Magic of Style* and benefit from the ideas presented.

Larisa Kronfeld

CONTENTS
• • • • •

Introduction

My philosophy for fashion and style is simple. What we women wear and how we look in our clothes matters, and should matter, to all of us ladies. Most women believe that they know how to dress stylishly, attractively and in good taste. However, my own observations suggest the opposite. Many, regardless of age and social status, could improve the way they dress significantly! Some require only minor adjustments; some need more substantial changes; while others actually are what I call "fashion victims."

For me, fashion and style have always been interesting and fun. I have never worked in the fashion industry nor taken any fashion classes. However, I have spent a lifetime being very intrigued and observing how clothes can help a woman attract more attention and look more appealing. Personally, I like to wear clothes that make me look more beautiful and also like to know that people notice.

As a Russian who grew up in the Soviet Union, I was unaware of anything involving fashion during my formative years. I was not even aware that "fashion" existed. However, when I was a little girl I would nag my mom incessantly to make my dresses because I didn't want to look like

7

everyone else. This was during a time when Soviet factories made clothes that used the same material and styles for everyone.

The selection of styles and colors was not large. Once you bought a dress, it wasn't unusual, as you walked down the street, to see three other women wearing the same dress. I'm not kidding! I believe this is when my desire began to stand out from among the rest.

I have a true passion for shopping and for finding different items, then mixing and matching them to create different looks. My observations and recommendations most likely are different from those you may have heard or read in the past. They are, in fact, specifically designed to help you identify how to look your best with the clothes that are most appropriate for you as an individual — that means clothes that compliment your body type and shape; go well with your skin complexion and hair color; and reflect your personal taste and comfort zone. If you follow my advice, you too can gain significant positive attention from men and women alike without necessarily spending a fortune in the process!

With so many books published about fashion and style, you may wonder why I saw a need to write this book and whether, indeed, it can really offer additional distinctive value. Well, in recent years, I have read many fashion books and magazines — so many, I could fill a small library with them! Yet, I haven't found anything that adequately addressed all I was looking for or needed. Most magazines depict beautiful clothes on beautiful models but offer little useful information for those who don't have model-perfect figures. Many of the published books attempt to be more relevant and provide more practical recommendations related to fashion, style and clothing. Some actually introduce interesting ideas and make good observations, but, unfortunately, they greatly over-generalize and over-simplify recommendations to the point of providing little value to us as individuals. In addition, I have yet to see a book that covers, in a comprehensive manner, all the different dimensions and topics that a woman needs to understand about how to use clothing to look more appealing. Of course, there also are the books written by celebrities who discuss how cool it is to be surrounded by designers who shower them with their latest designs. Unfortunately, this does not apply to those of us who live in the real world — those who don't have perfect figures, don't get expensive clothes for free, and can't look like a movie star everywhere we go.

This book is meant for all of us "real" women! Its purpose is to teach you all about how to work best with who you are, what you have and what you can afford.

Whether we're students heading to a class, or adults meeting friends for lunch or heading to work, we can always look great no matter what the occasion.

You may ask how a book like this can help you. As I share my observations, knowledge and experience regarding fashion and style, my hope is that my insights will make you much wiser and more discerning.

In this book I will share with you my smallest and biggest secrets about fashion and style and demonstrate how they can impact your everyday life. I will teach you very practical ways, by which you can enhance your personal style, look your best and make the most of your current wardrobe. I hope the photos and tips included in this book will inspire you to make adjustments that will make you more captivating. I also will share with you my own fashion mistakes in the hope that you don't go down that same unfashionable path. If you follow my advice, the stylish woman inside you will wisely emerge. You will identify and hone in your style instincts and become more confident that you are looking your best. Dressing with style will become a habit.

This book will also help you discover the true meaning of fashion and style, as well as help you learn how not to be a fashion victim. You certainly have seen such examples like the women who parade around in designer clothes, but who just don't look pulled together, or worse, look ridiculous in them. You'll also understand why fashion and style should be important and how you can use them to your advantage.

Do you know what colors work for you? I'll help you answer that question, as well as provide advice about the best way to shop in your quest for style. You will learn all you need to know regarding every major clothing item: pants, shorts, skirts, dresses, tops and blouses, plus evening wear — including formal and informal, jackets and coats. I will also provide insights into how to best use different accessories: scarfs, bags, shoes, purses, etc. You'll also better understand what kinds of clothing flatter your body type for every occasion. This entire process can be fun and exciting. Get ready to present yourself with the confidence that you appear alluring to the world!

I'll show you how to organize your closet to make it work for you. It will no longer be the "Bermuda Triangle" … where things disappear and cannot be found. This will help you save time getting ready and assist you in your efforts to look great, too!

I will also point out some behavioral traits that impact on how attractively you come across. In other words, The Magic of Style will teach you all you need to know about how to maximize your appeal and with it, your own confidence level when you interact with people.

Yours,
Larisa Kronfeld

Chapter 1

HOW DO WE FORM OPINIONS ABOUT FASHION AND STYLE?

How do we learn about fashion and style? We learn about them throughout our lives. As children we learn by observing our mothers, sisters, friends and neighbors. We listen to the advice they give each other and to us. We get feedback through comments people make about each other and about ourselves, as we dress to impress. Like everything else, the knowledge and style habits we acquire in childhood stay with us into adulthood, consciously or subconsciously. Unless our mothers, neighbors and friends worked as editors at Vogue or another fashion publication, most of us acquired and helped propagate many bad habits and a poor understanding of fashion and style.

If you are like me, you probably believe that you have become more discerning about fashion and style from reading various fashion magazines. Those magazines were my bible. I read them and immediately went out to buy the clothes they claimed were in fashion.

Probably, like me, you believed that you could count on those magazines to learn all you need to know about fashion and style. If I only focused as much on my school work as I did on those magazines, I would have become a much better student and maybe end up at Harvard!

However, in reality, the beautiful, colorful fashion magazines may teach us about fashion, but do not really teach us much about style and taste. They have a different objective — promote the fashion industry and make money in the process!

13

In other words, magazines are businesses like any other business, with the main goal of making a profit. This is neither good nor bad; it is just reality! Magazines are another form of selling entertainment and catching audience interest. Their goal is for readers to buy more magazines, which will enable them to make more money from advertisers. You, undoubtedly, already have realized it too by now. How many times have you tried on something shown in a magazine that didn't work for you? If you are like me, most likely, this happened many times. What looked gorgeous on a model just didn't look quite as good on you. Possibly, you have a different body shape or skin tone, or your age is different. Also, what looks good on the runway or red carpet may not look appropriate in real life situations.

*I*am sure they thought that they were dressed attractively.

Looks like a cabbage, as it has too many layers and is a mismatch of items and colors.

This combination of a summer silk skirt, wool pantyhose and a fur coat don't mix well, and the red shoes are the wrong color for her outfit.

This outfit displays too many colors everywhere — on the dress, the bag and on the shoes.

Really? Her bra shows through her dress! And she is carrying a Tiffany bag at the same time!

This summery, light, colorful dress does not go with the heavy, dark boots.

"LUXURY MUST BE COMFORTABLE OTHERWISE IT IS NOT LUXURY."
· · · · · COCO CHANEL · · ·

Striving to fit magazine images of a "fashionable" woman doesn't normally work all that well for most of us. For many, it subconsciously brings up some inferiority complex, while, for others, it may even result in frustrations and the conclusion that the world of fashion and style is "just not for me." We subconsciously feel inferior and uncomfortable. Over time, we may even detach from fashion and style as a self-defense mechanism. Yet, the normal and healthy desire to look pretty and be stylish still lives within us all. Worse yet, after many failed attempts to replicate what we see in fashion spreads and on red carpet coverages, some actually begin to convince themselves that looks do not matter. To make ourselves feel better, we even resort to the wonderful expression, "A book shouldn't be judged by its cover." While true in many situations, it is not the case with fashion and style. Let's be honest. We each judge all books by their covers! If the cover is not appealing, we are not likely to give it a second glance.

*H*ow We Dress Is Very Important!

It is a reality of life that people treat us differently based on how we dress. As much as we would like to believe otherwise, we live in a world where we are dependent on other people, how they view us and how they treat us. Style is an important element in how people perceive us. Don't ignore this fact; use it to your advantage!

In a later chapter I will discuss how being dressed well and dressed properly actually increases self-confidence. I also will explain how your attire affects how you come across to people and how they react to you. You'll be amazed at the difference it makes.

Also, if you dress inappropriately, you may evoke the wrong reactions, even from acquaintances. Do you remember when you met a person socially and he or she came dressed inappropriately for the occasion? They probably appeared inconsiderate and disrespectful to you, and you probably got insulted because they didn't appear to have taken the time to "prepare" for the meeting with you, which left you believing that you were not important enough for them to have done otherwise.

*W*orse yet, how did you feel when you threw a "formal" or special party that you spent months preparing for? You worked hard to achieve just the right atmosphere, and then someone showed up as if that person just returned from the beach. I would imagine you felt hurt and insulted, if not worse! Think about it and show your respect to others by how you dress.

17

Becoming More Insightful About Fashion and Style

I don't mean to suggest that fashion magazines have no value. Many times they offer great ideas, show beautiful clothes and make great observations. They provide a great way to learn about the principles of fashion and the fact that clothes, indeed, have impact on peoples' perception of us.

However, remember to take what you read with a "grain of salt" when you look for inspiration in magazines. By design, magazines must appeal to the largest possible audience. Their advice and observations are, by necessity, general in nature. It would be impossible to provide individualized observations, even when they claim otherwise. Be aware of this so you don't just blindly mimic what you see! Think of those magazines as free lesson for teaching you the basics of fashion and style. However, keep in mind that you are still responsible for individualizing them for yourself.

Watching movies and TV shows is another effective way to learn more about fashion and style. Hollywood does have the best costume and clothing designers and stylists in the world. We can learn much from what we see on the screen. It offers a great opportunity for insights and awareness about how clothes can enhance a woman's looks and make us cognizant of age-appropriate clothes and styles.

All Gates →

Chapter 1: How Do We Form Opinions About Fashion and Style?

$\mathcal{R}$ecognize that dressing in style does indeed achieve the intended result if done well!

For example, the wonderful costume designer, Patricia Field, did an amazing job of styling the actors for the movie, *The Devil Wears Prada*. Each character looked exquisitely stylish and the clothes perfectly fit each character's age. Field also did a marvelous job on the show *Sex in the City*, whose characters quite deservingly have actually become style icons around the world. Think also of the fabulous and stylish clothes worn by Julia Roberts in *Pretty Woman*, created by the famous costume designer Marilyn Vance-Starker, and those created by Edith Head for Audrey Hepburn's character in *Breakfast at Tiffany's*.

You can learn a lot from movies, particularly from what appeals to you and what doesn't. But, understand that you need to consider for yourself whether the observations you made would also apply to you. Draw the appropriate conclusions from both good and bad! Personally, I learned an enormous amount from movies. The trick is to observe carefully and apply what you see to the way you dress and the choices you make. You may be surprised by the result. Of course, my hope is to provide you the benefit of my years of studying, observing and analyzing what is, and what is not, appropriate at an individual level.

Magazines, movies and television are easy and a fun way by which to study the principles of fashion and style. However, there is a better, more entertaining way to accomplish this same result and much more — through field work and your own power of observation. Use this technique; there is nothing like it! Just take a look around wherever you are — in a restaurant, a shopping mall or even walking in the streets. If you watch carefully, you will see many different women; some will be dressed well and some poorly.

BREAKFAST AT TIFFANY'S

PRETTY WOMAN

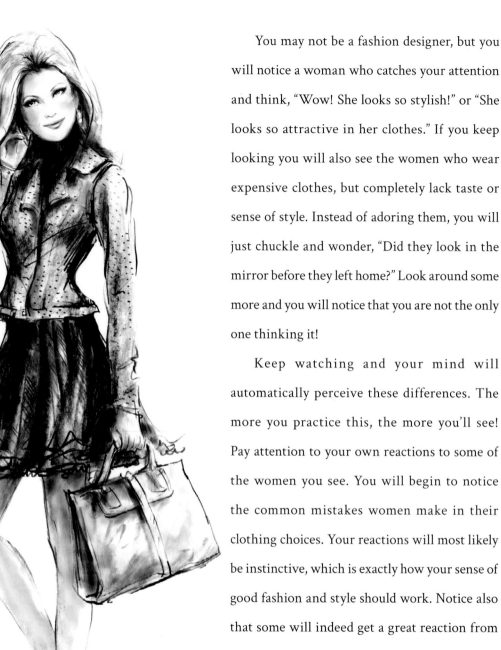

You may not be a fashion designer, but you will notice a woman who catches your attention and think, "Wow! She looks so stylish!" or "She looks so attractive in her clothes." If you keep looking you will also see the women who wear expensive clothes, but completely lack taste or sense of style. Instead of adoring them, you will just chuckle and wonder, "Did they look in the mirror before they left home?" Look around some more and you will notice that you are not the only one thinking it!

Keep watching and your mind will automatically perceive these differences. The more you practice this, the more you'll see! Pay attention to your own reactions to some of the women you see. You will begin to notice the common mistakes women make in their clothing choices. Your reactions will most likely be instinctive, which is exactly how your sense of good fashion and style should work. Notice also that some will indeed get a great reaction from you, while others will not.

Clothes and how we wear them do catch attention. They help differentiate us and can make us look more beautiful, classy and elegant!

$\mathcal{F}$inally, recognize that fashion and style do not necessarily need to be expensive.

Is expensive better? Sometimes, but not necessarily. Some women believe that the more expensive and trendy clothes will indeed make them look more stylish and chic; however, they just end up looking ridiculous. These are the "fashion victims" who do not have any idea what style is. They buy expensive, trendy clothes, but are clueless regarding whether these clothes really enhance their looks. Interestingly, these same clueless women are certain they look more beautiful, classy and elegant just because their clothes are expensive and have a designer label. That's wrong! Designer clothes and big price tags do not automatically make someone stylish, nor are these clothes suited to everybody.

I am reminded of my early years growing up in the Soviet Union. Russian women have a well-deserved reputation for being very mindful of individual style and dressing to enhance their looks. Keep in mind, however, that when I was a child in the Soviet Union, the country didn't have much to offer in terms of clothing selection or individuality, yet most women learned to be stylish with only the essentials. I guess I was a fashion "child prodigy," as I acquired the fashion bug very early in life.

As a child, even though I had to wear a uniform to school, I thought that I would die if I looked like everybody else. I needed to be special. The uniform was brown, but I wanted a blue one, which was allowed, but was nowhere to be found. This color was rarely available and very difficult to find. As you probably guessed, I was the one student out of thousands who found and wore a blue uniform. My mother searched for it for almost two years; it was only after she had found it that I finally stopped nagging.

Even though Russian women have always been style-savvy, they also could become fashion victims. When the Soviet Union broke up, designer fashions started pouring in. I remember how everyone got so excited and felt "enlightened" by the new clothes and magazine images. This was the "new Russia" and, as Russian women go, nobody would outdo them! Suddenly, everything was overdone to the point of being funny. They all began to wear Versace, Gucci and Dolce & Gabbana (D&G). The quantity and variety of those clothes at first were quite limited, but no one seemed to care. They bought whatever was available whether it fit well, was the right size, or with any thought of whether or not it looked good on them. The only thing that mattered was that they were wearing clothes that had a designer label. Everybody showed admiration — not for the woman, but rather for those designer clothes; not for how she looked in them, but for the fact that she could have afforded them!

It was humorous! Interestingly, all those who could afford it also believed that whatever they wore made them look stylish and more attractive. After all, they were wearing the newest designer brands and styles.

I guess they missed the subtlety of the difference between how great the dress looked versus how great the woman looked in that dress. You can only imagine the number of the poorly dressed women who spent a fortune on trying to look attractive but ended up looking ridiculous! If it weren't funny, it would have been sad! It took a number of years for the initial craze over designer clothes to subside and before things got back to normal, but its lessons were not lost on me and should not be on you either.

About eight years ago, I arrived in the United States full of admiration for anything American. Many times, however, when I noticed women and how they dressed, I felt like I had been transported back to the Soviet Union in the era of the initial discovery of designer clothes.

Designer clothes in the United States are everywhere! Many women wear them, but, way too often, they wear them in poor taste, lacking style! Rather than the clothes working to enhance their looks, they often detract from them. Yet, these women seem unaware of this, fed by people around them who keep giving them empty compliments, which they completely believe! This is how I learned about the frequent superficiality of the American compliments.

Compliments are everywhere and are easily given. Socially, Americans prefer to make the people around them feel good. There is nothing wrong with that. Actually, it is a wonderful trait. Why criticize someone if it concerns something that is not important? Why make somebody feel bad unnecessarily?

Americans understand this well and frequently apply this understanding to properly place the compliments they receive in the right perspective and rarely just blindly accept such compliments as reflecting the total truth. However, when it comes to clothing and appearances, they seem to completely forget about the superficiality and absolutely, totally believe these compliments. Unfortunately, this serves to mistakenly reinforce in their own minds that their clothing choices are effective and so they continue to make the same mistakes and never learn the truth. Again, if it was not sad, it would be funny! These women probably just confuse the "admiration" they receive for their ability to afford expensive clothes, from whether these clothes indeed are appropriate for the occasion and make them look more beautiful, and classy.

*L*et's remember these three words: *appropriate*, more *beautiful* and *classy*.

Finally, as I mentioned earlier, the journey to become a fashion and style "maven" is a never-ending process, since fashion and style constantly change and new do's and don'ts apply. For some, this journey will seem easy, while others will find it more difficult and frustrating.

Regardless, persevere and you will surely see results before too long. Look at this experience as fun and entertaining and the length and difficulty of the journey will bother you much less. I promise you one thing: I'll teach you everything you need to know and understand about good fashion and style. If you do your part and keep observing and learning, you will automatically, naturally become good at it, and it will forever be fun! The power of observation is indeed magical and transforming. As the lyrics of the song in the movie *The Devil Wears Prada* say, "... Suddenly I see, this what I wanna be!"

Chapter 2

> "ART PRODUCES UGLY THINGS WHICH FREQUENTLY BECOME BEAUTIFUL WITH TIME. FASHION, ON THE OTHER HAND, PRODUCES BEAUTIFUL THINGS WHICH ALWAYS BECOME UGLY WITH TIME."
> ····· JEAN COCTEAU ···

FASHION VS. STYLE

In the first chapter, I used the words "fashion" and "style" together as if they were one and the same, but they are really not. Many people confuse the two. As a result, they believe they are indeed the same and often use them interchangeably. I wouldn't be surprised to learn that the fashion industry "helped" our misunderstanding and confusion as they most benefit from the confusion and have the most to gain. Think about it. If fashion and style are the same, then, if fashion changes constantly, you must constantly buy new things to stay fashionable and stylish. Have you noticed how quickly fashions change? The more it changes the more you must buy and the more money the industry makes. It has gotten to be ridiculous. Even the weather doesn't change as drastically and as frequently as fashion.

*Even the dictionary knows better. The dictionary defines **fashion** as "a practice, or interest that is very popular for a short time." Yet, **style** is defined as "a particular kind, sort, or type, as with reference to form, appearance, or character." Can you see the difference? Fashion is a short-term practice, or interest, while style is not limited by time and refers directly to form, appearance and character.*

Fashion

As the dictionary suggests, fashion and style are not the same. They may be complementary and enhance each other, but not necessarily; they may work together, but not all the time.

. . . . .

In other words, fashion, by definition, is a fad and temporary, while style reflects long-term character and appearance!

. . . . .

Fashion comes and goes, while style stays with you forever. Fashion easily becomes "old-fashioned," while style maintains its freshness. Fashion in its current form has been "sold" to us and has really become just another social game for adults!

Chapter 2: Fashion vs. Style

Have you noticed? New fashion collections are introduced every three months. They are here today gone tomorrow. Yet, we are the ones stuck with the clothes we no longer can wear! Your closet ends up looking like a museum! I guess that is why, when the fashion industry introduces a new line, they call it a new "collection!"

Now, please understand, I don't mean to ill speak about fashion. It does introduce beautiful new clothes, forms and colors. There is nothing wrong with playing the game of being fashionable and trendy. It gives us a sense of being socially acceptable and can be comforting to many. If you can afford it (or have a great husband who can), then you may even get other women to be envious! That is, not envious of how you look, rather envious of your ability to afford it! Making people envious of you because of your ability to afford beautiful, more expensive things has its own social value. It implies that you are a successful person, which causes people to show you more respect and give you more deference — at least outwardly. However, this is a different game than looking more attractive. If this is what you want to achieve, then the more power to you. Enjoy the game of fashion!

$\mathscr{S}$tyle

Style is a different game! I feel sorry for the women who buy expensive designer clothes then parade around like peacocks, believing that they look great in them. True, some women wear them with great style, but many others look ridiculous, displaying no style, taste or class. People actually wind up chuckling rather than admiring.

Style should accomplish just the opposite. Learn to be stylish and you can play the game of fashion even more effectively by combining the two in a complementary and powerful way. But, this starts with style and not fashion. You should strive to be stylish, not fashionable. It is your **style** that defines you, your appearance and character. This is where you want to focus your attention.

The Transformative Power of Style

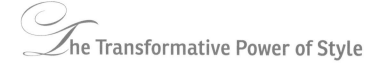

Style is more than showing who you are. It actually can transform your image to radiate who you want to be and how you want to be perceived. In other words, fashion is dependent and is defined by designers, while style is defined entirely by you and for yourself!

The end result of good style is the three magic words I mentioned earlier: more **beautiful**, **classy** and **appropriate** for the occasion. Remember, this doesn't necessarily mean more expensive. You don't have to be a millionaire to look like a million dollars!

Style also provides an added bonus that may seem counter-intuitive, but is quite true: when you seek fashion your selection is more limited, influenced by only what is fashionable at the moment. However, when you instead dress for style, your selection is unlimited. Therefore, avoid buying fashionable and trendy clothes for the sake of fashion. Instead, buy those fashionable clothes that are also stylish and represent who you are; they will last for a much longer time.

The Magic of Style by Larisa Kronfeld

I have a favorite expression: fashion should work for you — not you for the fashion industry! I can assure you that you will find clothes more than ten years old in my closet that I keep wearing. I receive new compliments every time I wear them, and nobody has ever accused me of not being fashionable!

Chapter 3

> "THE GOAL I SEEK IS TO HAVE PEOPLE REFINE
> THEIR STYLE THROUGH MY CLOTHING WITHOUT
> HAVING THEM BECOME VICTIMS OF FASHION."
> · · · · · GIORGIO ARMANI · · ·

WHAT IS YOUR STYLE?

What does it mean to have your own style? What truly looks good on you and enhances your looks, rather than what looks good on a model? What makes you feel most confident that you look your best at all times, not just for special occasions? How many times have people, or magazines, tried to tell you what your style should be, how you should find one, or improve it? How many times have you noticed how the cover pages of magazines try to entice you to buy those magazines with the promise that, if you take the test printed inside, you will learn what your style really is, or should be? Better yet, how many times have you taken those tests and actually believed them — or laughed at the results?

Remember, these are the exact same magazines that claim to tell you what every woman would love to know: "The 10 Things that Men Like Most." I hope by now you have learned the obvious truth: there are no ten men who like the same things! So why do those magazines continue to do it? Apparently, the technique sells the magazines! These are the same magazines that promise to help you find your style, which is as effective as promising to reveal the ten things men like the most. Remember, magazine publishers are in business for the money, and they make money by catching your attention and convincing you to buy what they advertise.

> *These magazines are like politicians. They promise a lot, rarely deliver, conveniently forget and repeat the whole cycle over and over again.*

Developing Your Personal Style

I hope that you will allow me to help you define your style in a simple way that will be most valuable to you. First and foremost, your style is **the clothes that make YOU feel comfortable, happy and confident**. It's not difficult to figure out that your favorite clothes are, therefore, your style! If suits are your favorite attire and your closet has more of them then other type of clothing, then that is your style. I'd call it "business style." If you love to wear jeans and T-shirts, and you purchase more of these to wear than anything else, then this is your style, which I call a "sporty style." If you like feminine dresses and high heels, then this is your style — a "romantic style." See how simple it is? I named them for you, but the name is not important. The style is your style, name it whatever you wish!

Keep in mind that identifying your style doesn't mean that you don't wear anything else. It just means that you prefer one style more than any other. Ask yourself: "What do I like to wear?" and "What kinds of clothes dominate my closet?" Congratulations! If you can answer these questions, you have identified your personal style. Accept and love it, because it is your exclusive style you created for yourself according to your personality. Please don't take any tests about "how to find your style?" or similar nonsense. Nobody from the outside can, or should, help you "find" it. You already have defined your true style. It's hanging in your closet.

*R*emember, style is an individual thing that should not be replaced by generalized tests, or guidelines that address a large audience. Instead, trust your own instincts!

Learn how to work with and within **YOUR** own true style to accomplish the desired outcome of becoming more beautiful, classy and appropriate. Your style may change with time, but it will keep you from becoming a fashion victim as it helps you stay within your comfort zone. However, style doesn't mean that you wear the same clothes all the time; if you do that, you will always look the same, which is something best to avoid. "Different" looks are preferred and are desirable in fashion and style.

Remember, style is a conceptual idea – comfortable, happy and confident. You can achieve different looks by just making small changes from one day to the next.

One more thing: If it is in your closet, but you don't use it, it is not your style! Your style is what you **wear**, not what you buy or collect!!! If you buy something but don't wear it, you may have been influenced by the outside world to believe that it will make you more stylish; then you have just become a fashion victim! Follow your instincts! You have the power! Work with your style. Don't stray and you'll enjoy it throughout your life.

Russians have an expression that wisely captures the essence of it all: "Habit is a form of life." In other words, keep thinking about what you put on and combine different ideas and looks. Before too long that will become a habit, feel natural and comfortable; it also will surely become part of your life.

Chapter 4

STYLE IS A WAY OF LIFE!

Many women think that to be stylish means to dress well only for special occasions. This myth is another byproduct of the fashion industry, which continually bombards us with the idea that being fashionable and stylish means special occasions that require special clothes. How can you believe that wearing an occasional beautiful dress but neglecting your looks at all other times makes you fashionable and stylish? Remember what I told you in the previous chapter? You wear stylish clothes to feel happy and comfortable, as well as to come across as more beautiful, classy and appropriate. Why? Because this is how you catch attention, differentiate yourself from others and influence your environment to your advantage. Why reserve it just for special occasions? Do you think that no one is looking at you or needs to be influenced the rest of the time? More importantly, if looking more beautiful, classy and appropriate makes you feel confident and happy, why reserve these feelings for only a few special occasions? Why not experience them all the time?

39

Personal Style Is What You Feel and How You Look

What if I told you that style is no more expensive than your budget allows and is very easy to accomplish? Don't be brainwashed by the fashion industry. When you start playing by their rules, you have just lost your personal style! The industry promotes "fashion" and "fashionable" as the key operative words. Wrong! The words fashion and fashionable are meaningless! **Stylish should be the magic word, and your personal style should be at the center of being stylish.**

Allow me, at this point, to give you a more descriptive definition of personal style that is easy to remember and is not just a concept. It will become your best guide when you buy and dress. You can probably guess this definition by now, as I keep emphasizing it. Nevertheless, here it is:

. . . . .

Personal Style

consists of the clothes you wear at any given time that not only

make you feel **comfortable**, **happy** and **confident**,

but also make you look more

beautiful, **classy** and **appropriate** for the occasion.

. . . . .

Please notice that there are two operative words in my definition: "make you **feel**" and "make you **look**." Both are significant as they involve the two most important players in this game — you, and the rest of the world. If you feel comfortable, happy and confident, you will exude it and people will notice and admire you. If you look more beautiful, classy and appropriate for the occasion, people will notice and keep looking at you. Please note that my definition does not use the word "sexy." In fact, sexy is the **wrong** look! If you look more beautiful, classy and appropriate, then most men will also consider you sexier, or "sexy." However, this does not necessarily work in reverse; if you dress to look "sexy," you may not look more beautiful, classy and appropriate. In fact, men may find you interesting only in this single dimension, which is only good if you are looking for a one night stand!

I hope you will agree that this is easy-to-follow advice. Congratulations! You are now ready to win this game! Go ahead and savor every moment of it! You deserve it!

Allow me to make another important observation and define the difference between style and being stylish from my perspective. The definition of style provided above does not address the element of time. Even though you can dress with style at any single time, "being **stylish**" means **being a person of style at all times**. In other words, being stylish is not accomplished by dressing well for a few special occasions; rather, it is a way of life! To be stylish and beautiful means to look your best every single day! Would you not prefer it this way if I also told you that it is easy and not any more expensive?

"THE ONLY RULE IS DON'T BE BORING
AND DRESS CUTE WHEREVER YOU GO.
LIFE IS TOO SHORT TO BLEND IN."

· · · · · PARIS HILTON · · ·

Chapter 5

STYLE FOR ALL OCCASIONS AND ALL TIMES

Your personal style should reflect and be appropriate for all occasions in which you find yourself. More importantly, your closet should mirror this with the right proportions. In other words, your closet should contain more of the clothes appropriate for the environments in which you will find yourself more frequently.

Wardrobe

The types and quantity of the clothes in your closet should directly reflect your daily life. If you work in an office every day, you should own more work-appropriate outfits than casual or formal wear. Your closet should contain the amount of clothes proportionate to the number of different occasions for which they will be worn. For example, if you spend 60 percent of your time in the office, then 60 percent of your wardrobe should be office-appropriate.

At the same time you should have enough clothes for all other occasions you may find yourself in. This way you will not only maximize the value of your clothes, but also, feel more comfortable, confident and noticed at all times and in all the right places.

Allow me to demonstrate in practical terms what personal style really is and how easy it is to achieve. I will use for this purpose what I call the "student style" because, at first glance, it may appear to be perplexing and impossible to achieve on campus, since most students have limited means and often look and dress similarly.

"I don't understand how a woman can leave the house without fixing herself up a little — if only out of politeness. And then, you never know, maybe that's the day she has a date with destiny. And it's best to be as pretty as possible for destiny."
· · · · · **Coco Chanel** · · ·

When I first came to America and attended school, I discovered that most students dressed alike, wearing jeans and T-shirts or tank tops in the summer and jeans and sweaters in the winter. Personal grooming was minimal. This student style is quite acceptable and appropriate for the occasion and that environment. Now, you may wonder about how one can appear stylish in such an environment without looking ridiculous and out of place.

Well, here is my next secret for you: it is quite possible and quite simple. Better yet, no one will think that you don't conform to the student style, yet they will all notice you more without even realizing it. Just follow my rule about the proportions of your closet and don't own only a single pair of jeans to use all the time.

First, your closet should reflect the fact that you are a student who spends the majority of her time in and around campus with other students. Therefore, at least half the clothes in your closet should fit in with the student style. Mostly, your wardrobe should consist of typical student clothing like jeans, tank tops, T-shirts, sweaters, sneakers, simple shoes, some winter scarves, and the like. You can achieve different looks by having a variety of these simple clothes. For example, Jeans and T-shirts could look more casual, classy, sexy, fancy, trendy, etc. Mix and match the pieces daily depending upon your mood, and viola, you look different every day! For the winter months, you can accomplish the same by mixing and matching sweaters and scarves.

45

Remember, the clothes don't have to be new to accomplish the desired effect; older clothes work just as well if you keep them looking clean and neat.

The same principle that works for students in school also applies to other environments. The wardrobe for a housewife, for example, should include a variety of blouses, nice pants, nice jeans, tops, both simple and fancy shoes, daily dresses, wrap-dresses, jackets — all simple to wear, but all very attractive. If you mix and match these according to your mood, you will achieve different looks all the time. Don't forget to notice the subconscious impact you have on your husbands and boyfriends; they **will** react — guaranteed!

*I*n other words, don't stray too much, but with a few small changes, you can accomplish a great deal of diversity for your overall looks. Again, the objective is to appear more beautiful, classy and appropriate, but **in subtle ways**.

In the workplace, use proper attire that appropriately reflects your office and company image. The principle is still the same. Own a variety of clothes that you can mix and match to enable you to achieve different looks. However, avoid trying to appear too obviously different from everyone else in that environment.

While appearing "different" is generally a positive for a woman, it may not be the case at work. The business environment requires teamwork and acceptance of corporate philosophy. Unfortunately, in this environment, your career is very dependent on how others perceive you. People will accept and like you more if you "fit the mold." Therefore, wear clothes that make you look more attractive, but in subtle ways and always appropriate for the environment! Trust me; this practice is wise and will reap big dividends.

Chapter 5: Style For All Occasions and All Times

Chapter 6

OBSERVATIONS AND GENERAL RULES ABOUT PERSONAL STYLE

Now that you understand how style should be reflected in the clothes you own, it is time to discuss what you need to do in order to transform yourself and become truly stylish.

The Seven Rules of Personal Style

There are some key rules that you need to keep in mind while learning the art of becoming stylish.

First rule - **Style**, not fashion, comes first! Fashion is an enhancer that allows for a double bonus play. So, if you enjoy also being "fashionable" then go ahead and do it. However, fashion should complement and enhance your style, not the other way around.

Second rule - As you mix and match clothing items, don't be afraid to experiment and try something new. Don't be afraid to break some "fashion rules" from time to time as they don't necessarily work all the time or for all women. Your test for breaking fashion rules should be internal. Ask yourself if you feel more comfortable with this look. Do you feel more beautiful, classy and appropriate? If so, then go ahead; you are on safe ground.

49

Third rule - Be mindful that your style, no matter what it is, always should reflect your lifestyle, habits, taste, status and age. Note the age thing! Way too many of us try to hang on to our more vibrant years. While it is great to stay young in body and spirit, it does not always work well with clothing and style. When a woman dresses inappropriately for her age, she is frequently subjected to ridicule, either openly or subtly. The British have actually coined an expression to describe this kind of woman and refer to her as "Mutton dressed as lamb." Unfortunately, in this department, many of us hang on for much too long. This may be due to wishful thinking, or just the desire to hold-on to and perhaps re-live the wonderful days we have left behind. Nevertheless, it is best to avoid doing so, regardless of circumstances.

Forth Rule - Although each woman should have her own individual style, it should always adapt and be appropriate to the current situation or setting. The whole purpose of your clothing and style is to communicate something to people — consciously and subconsciously. This communication, both verbal and nonverbal, becomes much more readily accepted if you, as an individual, seem to belong and be part of the group. In this case as well, the **subtle way is the better way; showing off is not well-received**.

Fifth rule - Black and white are "safe" and are good colors, but they are boring! Too many women are afraid to wear colors because they don't feel comfortable with their own sense of color. They understand that the wrong colors on them can ruin a great look and are afraid to take the risk. While it's true that one can rarely go wrong with the basic black and white, one could miss a great opportunity to look even better with the addition of colors. Don't be afraid to experiment! Add colors to your style and don't worry! Later in the book I will give you useful rules regarding colors that will enable you to make wiser choices.

Sixth rule - Keep observing and learning. You may not have the talent of a designer, but you certainly possess the instincts — we all do. Therefore, don't be discouraged and don't withdraw — clothes are important! Men may be blind to fashion, style and clothing, but women are not! Beauty is an intrinsic part of every woman and each woman wants to be noticed. Women are born with instincts that understand and differentiate beauty. These instincts have been taught, handed down and honed since the beginning of time. Trust me. This is largely true with very few exceptions. The only difference is that some women are more developed in this area, and some display exceptional talent when it comes to discerning and achieving beauty. It is important not to withdraw, give up, or downplay beauty's significance just because it may seem difficult at first. Remember, clothing and style are important elements in how people perceive us. Persevere and all this will become second nature to you as well. More importantly, amazing as it may sound, you will actually begin to enjoy it and feel more confident and beautiful. You have no need to worry, or be hesitant! Later in this book I will provide you with the understanding and the tools necessary to allow you to start your journey on firm footing.

Seventh rule - Remember the magic words: your personal style must be comfortable, make you more confident and make you look more beautiful, classy and appropriate.

Chapter 6: Observations and General Rules About Personal Style

Chapter 7

> "THERE IS MUCH TO SUPPORT THE VIEW THAT IT IS CLOTHES THAT WEAR US AND NOT WE THEM; WE MAY MAKE THEM TAKE THE MOULD OF ARM OR BREAST, BUT THEY WOULD MOULD OUR HEARTS, OUR BRAINS, OUR TONGUES TO THEIR LIKING."
> · · · · · VIRGINIA WOOLFE · · ·

DRESSING FOR STYLE

You probably have heard the expression "the means to an end" many times. In our case, clothes are the means and style is the end. In other words, dressing for style means using clothes that end up making you feel comfortable and confident, while at the same time making you look more beautiful, classy and appropriate. The first part is simple; you either feel it, or you don't. It depends entirely on you and you are the sole judge of the result. The second part is a bit trickier. There is a certain amount of art to it, plus some rules and guidelines. Most importantly, the end result for the second part is not **your** judgment, but rather, the judgment of others. This chapter will provide you many of the rules and guidelines you need to accomplish it. However, before we start, here is the over-arching rule you may want to follow:

Whatever you wear should:

- Build on your strong physical attributes and enhance them; and/or

- Camouflage your weaker physical attributes; and/or

- Attract attention to yourself in a soft and subtle way.

In other words, your clothes should work well to showcase your physical attributes. However, when you want to emphasize a positive physical attribute, do it in a subtle way. Subtlety is much more effective because people react to it subconsciously, which is the strongest and most desirable form of reaction. At the same time, by being subtle, you avoid the risk of being perceived as "flaunting" or "showing off," both of which evoke feelings of aversion and dislike. For example, if you want to draw attention to your breasts, show only a small amount of cleavage. Showing too much cleavage is less effective and, in the extreme, becomes distasteful. If you have a great figure, wear tighter outfits but avoid overly tight clothes so you don't come across as being too provocative or, in extreme cases, lewd. If you have great legs and you want to show them off, you might wear a shorter dress or skirt rather than a longer one, if and when also appropriate for the occasion. However, unless you are chronologically very young, don't overdo it. If you wear something that is too short, it is likely to backfire and you will be perceived as being unrefined, having poor taste and, if extremely short, even being vulgar. Also, please note that in the above examples the older chronologically you are the more acute the negative reactions.

Working with Physical Attributes

Only two types of physical attributes really matter when you discuss clothing and style: (a) overall figure and body proportions — I'll call it "body type" and; (b) skin, eyes and hair colors. Focus your attention on these and you'll gain a significant advantage in using clothes to your benefit. You guessed right! What might work for one figure, may not work for another. What may look good for one certain body type, may not look good on another. Colors that look right on one person, may not work for another due to different skin, eye and hair colors. Now you can better understand why the major operative word with style is **personal** style?

Chapter 7: Dressing for Style

Working with Different Body Types

There are three things we can state with certainty:

- Just like faces, most people have different body types.
- We each like some parts of our bodies and hate others.
- We are our own worst critics of our bodies.

Be that as it may, our bodies are ours; there is little we can do to change them! However, there is much we can do with clothes to enhance the parts we like and camouflage the parts we don't.

Body Proportions

In the past, you may have heard that what matters most about choosing the right clothes are your height and weight, followed by the shape of your overall body — whether pear or apple shape, or top- or bottom-heavy. You may have read about many do's and don'ts for tall versus short and for skinny versus overweight people, but are you ready for a revelation? My observation is quite contrarian. While the do's and don'ts about how to dress when you are tall, short, overweight, skinny, top-heavy or bottom-heavy are appropriate, except in very pronounced cases, they are **not** the most relevant. Rather, what matters most are the **relative proportions** of your body!

You may be very skinny and small-boned, but if your hips are relatively wider than your shoulders, then, by my definition, you have proportionately wider hips. Conversely, if your shoulders are relatively wider than your hips, you have proportionately wider shoulders. If you are plump, but have small chest, then your bust is proportionately smaller. If you are tall, but your legs are short in relation to your height, then you have proportionately shorter legs, and vice versa. You need to determine your own body type, including your strong and weak attributes and work with these to attain the best results. When you look into a mirror, try to focus on what about your body you most want people to notice and what you would prefer to camouflage. However, don't overlook the smaller, less obvious things, like a long or short neck relative to your body; fat or skinny arms relative to your body; fat or skinny calves relative to your body, etc.

This should clarify what I mean when I mention body types and proportions. Focus on your relative body proportions and you will become much more sophisticated in your choices and will do much better with selecting clothes that are best for you.

Chapter 7: Dressing for Style

General Observations and Guidelines Regarding Body Types

Before I provide the actual guidelines, I'd like you to take note of some key observations:

✓ These are just guidelines and not an exhaustive list of do's and don'ts, but they will put you on the path to understand the principles of how to choose clothes appropriate to your body type.

✓ These are guidelines, not rules; so experiment, try your own variations and discover new ones on your own, after you understand the principles.

✓ Many women will fit multiple categories of body types that I address below. If this is true for you, choose an appropriate combination under each category.

✓ You may already realize that if a certain guideline accomplishes something for you, then the opposite will accomplish exactly the reverse, on both the positive and negative sides. For example:

　* You may cover your arms because they are disproportionately fat, while if you leave them uncovered, you will emphasize them more;

　* If you have feminine and sexy arms, then you might want to leave them uncovered to emphasize them. If you cover them, you forego the opportunity to show them off.

✓ As a general rule, the more disproportionate one section of your body seems to be, the more noticeable it is likely to be, making it even more important to follow these guidelines.

By now, you probably can surmise that the principle behind these guidelines is quite simple; wear the types of clothes that reveal what you want people to see and obscure the parts you rather they not see, which I call the "direct way." However, there is another, more subtle way that is as effective to accomplish the same results, which I call it the "indirect way." Like a magician performing a trick, using the indirect way, you subtly "help" re-direct people's attention and eye focus away from what you don't want them to notice. Needless to say, if the eyes don't focus on something, then, by definition, it is not as noticeable. This is exactly what you want to happen!

GUIDELINES FOR WOMEN WHO ARE VERY TALL, SHORT, OVERWEIGHT OR SKINNY

If you are very tall, or short — or overly fat or skinny, you will be well-served to adhere to the following few guiding principles involving clothes to avoid, because they will tend to exaggerate such attributes.

Short Women

- Short women should avoid long jackets. They make them look even shorter!

- Short women should avoid clothing that is too loose. It only makes them appear short AND fat!

- Short women should avoid high-waisted pants and skirts. These make their tops look unattractive!

- Short women should avoid tops that display horizontal lines. Such lines make them look wider. Instead, whenever possible, they should choose to wear vertical lines, which make them look taller.

Tall Women

- Tall women should avoid short jackets. They will appear strange and unseemly!

- Tall women can get away with wearing loose clothing.

Overweight Women

Overweight women should avoid wearing tight clothes, including the "slightly" tight clothes that will be just perfect as soon as we lose a little weight, which we expect to happen very shortly. Keep in mind that we tend to naturally underestimate our own weight and how tight our clothes are on us. Be assured that they are much more noticeable by others and emphatically broadcast that you are fat! In particular, avoid tightly-fitted buttoned shirts and jackets that "burst open" at the buttons. The same goes for tight pants, particularly stretch pants.

GUIDELINES FOR OTHER BODY TYPES

Are your breasts proportionately large? If so,

- Clothes that do not cover your shoulders will redirect eyes away from your bosom to your shoulders.

- Clothes that have an open décolleté, but are not **too** low cut, will divert attention from your bust to your upper chest and neck. However, be careful not to wear a bra that squeezes your breasts!

- Avoid large and loose tops. Large tops may hide a large bust, but they will make you appear disproportionately fat!

- Wear bras that support and lift your breasts slightly. Large, loose boobs seem larger when not supported!

- Wear tops and sweaters that have up-to-down front buttons, but are not too tight.

- Wear tops that are darker in color than your bottoms.

- Avoid wearing big, wide belts as they will make you look even more top-heavy!

Is your bosom proportionately small? If so,

- Wear blouses or dresses with ruffles as this style is a great, subtle bust enhancer!

- Wear big scarves and a push-up bra. These are always good choices.

- Wear a high neckline. V-necklines and wraps are not for you. Choose to wear things that will redirect attention from your chest to other parts of your body. For example, try to emphasize your arms, shoulders or waist by wearing a wide belt. You may prefer to wear flared pants or fuller jeans rather than wearing pants that are tight.

Are your arms proportionately large, or fat? If so,

- Wear long-sleeved clothes when possible.

- Use scarves or shawls to cover the tops of your arms whenever possible.

- Avoid sleeveless clothes that expose your bare arms. Even partially covering your shoulders and the tops of your arms will accomplish visual miracles.

- Wear V-neck tops as a great way to redirect eyes away from your arms to your bust!

- Avoid wearing clothes that have sleeves that drape over the arms, as this draping draws more attention to the arms and exaggerates their appearance!

Are your shoulders proportionately wide? If so,

- Avoid jackets with padding, or just remove the pads, as padding makes shoulders appear bigger and wider!

- Avoid tight tops and sweaters where their sleeve seams start exactly at the end of the shoulders as this draws focus directly to the shoulders! Undetectable shoulder seams are the best choice to look for when selecting clothes.

- Avoid wearing V-necks since they will make your shoulders stand out more!

- Clothes that reveal part of your shoulders will make them look smaller. This will draw focus to the stark line on the shoulder created by the covered and uncovered parts, as opposed to the full shoulder. This will make your entire upper body appear narrower.

- Wear dark tops with lighter colored bottoms, as dark colors better mask problem areas.

- Wear high heels, or heavy platform shoes, which balance wide shoulders.

Are your legs proportionately long and your torso short? If so,

This may actually be a "good" problem. You probably may have heard the cliché that long legs are beautiful legs! Therefore, you may not want to conceal your long legs unless you feel like they make your upper body look too short. If that is the case, then:

- Wear flat shoes, rather than high heels.

- Avoid high-waisted clothes. Wear jeans, pants and skirts with a low waistline since a high waistline will make your legs appear even longer. Worse yet, a high waistline will make your upper body appear shorter!

- Wear cardigan sweaters with top-to-bottom buttons.

- Wear blouses, sweaters and jackets that are on the longer side to make your legs appear shorter and your upper body longer!

- If you have a nice chest, than you can use open neck and low neck cut tops to divert attention to your attractive bust!

- Wear V-line tops to make your torso look longer!

- Wear blouses and sweaters, untucked — on the outside of your pants or skirts to obscure the spot where the torso ends and legs begin!

- Use narrow belts and avoid "wild" or otherwise eye-catching belts. The waist is not where you want to draw focus!

Chapter 7: Dressing for Style

Are your legs proportionately short and your torso long? If so,

- Wear high heeled shoes if you can as high heeled shoes make legs appear longer!

- Wear skirts with high boots as wearing "normal" shoes with skirts only highlights and draws attention to your short legs!

- Avoid wearing ankle boots or your legs will look even shorter!

- Avoid wearing three-quarter length long pants as they exaggerate the problem!

- Wear high-waisted pants and skirts.

- Wear long pants whenever possible, but don't let them fold on themselves and drag over your shoes, or bunch up on the bottom.

- Avoid wearing jeans, or pants inside your boots as this emphasizes the disproportion!

- Wear lighter colored tops. They soften the contrast between the long torso and short legs.

- Wear tops that are on the shorter side as they make the torso appear shorter.

- Wear A-line dresses and skirts that widen near the bottom; this serves as a great camouflage for shorter legs!

- Wear short-cut jackets.

- Use "wilder" looking or eye-catching belts.

- Wear more dresses and skirts instead of pants.

Are your hips proportionately wider and your shoulders narrower? If so,

Since I share this problem with you, I can help you a lot due to my own extensive experimentation while trying to camouflage it.

- Wear clothes that are light colored on the top and darker on the bottom.

- Avoid wearing lighter colors around your buttocks than you wear on your upper body. If you want to wear lighter colors around your midsection, for whatever reason, than use a jacket or a long sweater to cover your butt.

- Wear tops with more aggressive colors or more complicated designs, paired with softer colored bottoms with simple designs.

- Wear straight skirts, pants or jeans.

- Wear A-line skirts and dresses.

- Wear jackets or sweaters that stop at your hips, or wear longer than average jackets.

- Wear scarves.

- Wear clothes that cover your shoulders, or clothes that make them appear wider.

- Avoid wearing wide skirts or pants unless they are made of a very light material, so as to avoid an appearance of a heavy, bulky look all around.

- Avoid wearing stretch jeans. If you do wear them, cover your butt with a long sweater or jacket, or wear your shirt on the outside of your pants.

- Avoid wearing short skirts as they make hips look bigger.

- Avoid clothes that coincidently make your hips look larger, like those with pockets, belts and other items which are worn around the hips.

- Wear straight-legged pants.

- Wear A-line or straight line skirts and dresses.

- Wear blouses and dresses with ruffles or draping at the top.

- Wear cardigans sweaters — those with top-to-bottom buttons.

- Avoid wearing heavy-looking or clunky platform shoes. Wear instead shoes that look lighter and have thin heels.

- Wear heavy or long necklaces as a great way to divert attention from the bottom of your body!

- Avoid loud, attention-catching belts. Use belts that complement or are the same color or tone as your pants, skirt or dress.

- Wear long jackets, sweaters, or cardigans that cover up your bottom.

- Avoid clothing with straight lines at the top and bottom as they exaggerate the problem!

68

*D*o you have a proportionately short neck? If so,

- Avoid turtlenecks or your small neck will completely vanish!

- Open your neck and bust a little to make your neck appear longer!

- Avoid wearing glass beads or pearls, especially around your neck, as they exaggerate the short look of your neck!

- Wear chains whenever possible, especially long ones.

- V-neck tops are a great look for you! You can wear long necklaces or open necklines easily. Cardigans and jackets where the top button is low and reveals more of your chest are best for you.

*I*s your stomach proportionately large? If so,

This is a tough one, because this is the one that causes people to mistakenly ask: "Are you pregnant?" Ouch!

- Avoid clothes that are snug around your stomach; they will make you look like a caterpillar!

- Avoid clothes that are tight, especially under your bust, or form a visible line under there as you really will appear to be pregnant!

- Wear low-waisted pants or jeans with wide tops. Strive to wear dark colors around your stomach and lighter colors elsewhere. This will focus attention on the lighter colors. Do not wear anything with a large pattern and avoid wearing a belt. A-line dresses will work very well for you.

*I*s your waist proportionately large? If so,

If your weight tends to concentrate around your waist, divert attention from your waist to your legs, shoulders or bust. To do this, you can:

- Wear A-line tops that widen toward the waist.

- Wear A-line skirts, but not along with an A-line top!

- Wear tops that are tight and make a visible line under your bra. This will accomplish the same result as an A-line top.

- Wear long jackets and avoid short ones.

- Wear a belt as, in most cases, it will help to better define your waist.

- Wear V-neck and deep open-neck tops to divert focus from the waist to the top!

*F*inally, are you a model? Do you have the figure of a model?

Do you have a model's figure and proportions? If so, you are a very lucky lady! You didn't need to read any of the above guidelines and may wear whatever you wish! As for me, and probably all other women, I envy you! However, just out of principle, I would like to offer you at least one observation. You may wear what you wish, however tight clothes that showcase your waistline would be a special "killer" for all the women around you. Enjoy it!

Sale

Chapter 8

> "TO CREATE SOMETHING EXCEPTIONAL,
> YOUR MINDSET MUST BE RELENTLESSLY
> FOCUSED ON THE SMALLEST DETAIL."
> · · · · · GIORGIO ARMANI · · ·

COLORS AND PERSONAL STYLE

Even if you are not an avid fan of fashion, I'll bet that you definitely have your favorite colors! To women, colors can be like breathing fresh air. Sadly however, many women really don't use colors very effectively or, worse yet, they use them poorly. The use of colors with clothes is actually more intricate than may seem. Some women seem to prefer clothes that are mostly black and white. While you can't go wrong with black and white, you can run the risk of looking "boring" after a while. I am a strong believer in the use of colors. Colors catch more attention, which is good for women; make us look less boring and more interesting, which is also good; and they make our lives more "colorful" — pun intended. If you are nervous about using colors or if you just prefer to wear black and white, at least consider injecting small items containing colors, like scarves, belts and tops. You will be surprised by how much more interesting you will look.

73

Basic Color Guidelines

Although all colors are good, some look better than others depending on the individual. As a result, you need to be aware of which colors work best for you and use them more frequently. Avoid using colors just because you liked them on other women as they may not fit you as well. It is best to find your own "right" colors. This chapter will provide you with some guidelines that will help you recognize which colors most likely will be especially effective for you and which might not. However, keep in mind that these are only suggestions and general guidelines. As I mentioned in previous chapters, ultimately, the best colors for you are your favorite colors and/or those you like naturally. They will be the ones that make you feel special and, more importantly, make you feel comfortable and confident. Remember, these colors are an important part of your personal style. You will know that you have found the best colors for you when some of your friends begin to say to themselves: "Wow, I should buy the same color blouse!" or scarf, or whatever!

Each basic color has a vast spectrum of different shades and tones from bright and strong all the way to soft and pastel. This offers you almost endless possibilities for colors to experiment with so you can discover which colors, shades and tones work best for you.

Every color can be categorized into two separate dimensions based on shade and tone. These are: Dark vs. Light and Warm vs. Cool

Dark colors, as the name suggests, have deeper, heavier color tones while light colors are the brighter and pastel-type colors.

Chapter 8: Colors and Personal Style

The warm vs. cool colors are not as obvious and readily apparent. They are differentiated based on whether they have more of a yellowish or bluish undertone. Those with a yellowish undertone are warm, while those containing a bluish undertone are cool. For example, look at any pure color like red, green or blue, and imagine mixing it with a shade of yellow. The original basic color changes when the yellow color is added. The end result becomes a shade with yellowish undertone referred to as a warm color. Now, imagine doing the same thing but adding a blue color. The end result will be a shade of the original color with a bluish undertone; this is then referred to as a cool color. Below is a simple visual illustration of the two categories using three basic colors: grey, red and yellow.

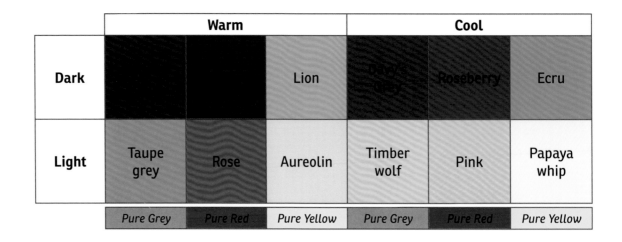

	Warm			Cool		
Dark			Lion	Dark grey	Roseberry	Ecru
Light	Taupe grey	Rose	Aureolin	Timber wolf	Pink	Papaya whip
	Pure Grey	*Pure Red*	*Pure Yellow*	*Pure Grey*	*Pure Red*	*Pure Yellow*

The above categorization provides the basis for my six most fundamental rules regarding color selection:

Which Colors Work Best for You?

The following six general rules will help you determine how to use colors to your utmost advantage:

Rule 1

Clothes will be more becoming if their colors match the color category of your hair, skin and eyes.

Rule 2

The colors you wear nearest your face are the most important ones. Those you wear further down from your face are of secondary importance. In other words, the colors of your shirt, sweater, jacket, etc., are more relevant than the colors of your pants, skirts or shoes. If your upper garment has multiple colors, then the color closest to your face is the most relevant. Therefore, based on rule one stated above, the color you wear at the very top should most closely match your hair, skin and eyes. Other clothing colors are not as critical, but should be compatible with the colors on top.

Rule 3

The color of your top outermost garment is the most important one. Therefore, if you wear a jacket, or a sweater, their colors become the more relevant while the color of your shirt becomes less so.

Rule 4

The colors in your scarf and/or hat, should you wear one, are very important as they are nearest to your face. A wrong color will ruin the overall effect.

Rule 5

The colors of your shoes, bags and accessories should be compatible with each other and with your clothes.

Rule 6

When mixing colors, dark colors generally mix better with other **dark** colors while **light** colors generally mix best with other **light** colors; mixing **dark** with **light** colors is more of a challenge. On the other hand, mixing **warm** and **cool** colors is not as problematic.

The following table will help you get started determining the best colors for you as an individual. The table contains basic recommendations for the colors of clothes that will match well with the more common hair, eyes and skin colors.

HAIR	EYES	SKIN	COLOR RECOMMENDATIONS
Any shades of blond	Blue Green Grey	Light, warm pinkish	Light colors are great for you. Avoid wearing dark colors. However, if you are going to wear a dark color, make sure it is combined with a light color like cream, ivory, light grey, sky blue, pastel pink, light cocoa, green apple, lavender or warm brown.
A golden-yellowish blond			Warm, energetic colors work very well for you. These include yellow-lemon, light peach, salmon coral, red, orange, Amaranth-red, magenta, rose, beaver-brown, caramel-brown, sunset, apple-green, royal blue and lavender. Recommended color combinations include Eton blue (derived from green) with Navajo white (derived from yellow), Prussian blue (a blue color) with apricot (an orange color); amethyst (a violet color) with indigo (a blue). These should be nearest to your face, although you may add additional colors anywhere below — even black, if you wish.
Whitish blond, and grey			Cool colors offer the best choice. These include eider white, comfort grey, purple, cooled blue, green, recycled, watery, pier, lemongrass, sea salt, coastal plain, nurture green, scanda, and rapture blue. If you want to mix colors, avoid aggressive colors since these colors are not as appropriate for you. The following color examples will work very well for you in a combination: comfort grey (a grey color) with mauve (from violet); and federal blue (a blue color) with sky blue (a cyan color). These colors should be located nearest to your face. If you want to add additional colors, even black, do so near the bottom of the garment.
Black Brown Red	Brown Green	Light brown to black	Dark colors like chocolate brown, lime, dark green, deep navy, purple and scarlet are great for you; black will be especially nice! You may mix them as you wish. However, if you wish to use light colors, make sure that you still include some dark colors. Limit your use of pastel colors.

HAIR	EYES	SKIN	COLOR RECOMMENDATIONS
Black Brown Red	Brown Green	Gold tone and/or light golden tan	Warm colors work best for you! You need to wear heavier colors rather than pale or pastel ones. These colors look powerful and elegant on you, especially olive, ecru, goldenrod, cooper, brown, sepia, avocado, dartmouth green, tea rose, bittersweet, fire brick, dark red and salmon pink. Major color combinations include medium taupe (a grey derivative) with bronze (a brown color); rose (a red color) with amaranth (a pink color); mint (a cyan color) with hunter green (a green color).
		Light whitish, or reddish, with blue undertone ("cool" color)	For you, cool colors work the best! Do not wear any warm colors at all! You can combine dark colors with cool colors. For example, Persian green, pine green, teal, magic mint, violet-blue, mahogany, redwood, cerise, Thulian pink all work well. Examples of some good color combinations include blue-grey (a grey color) with Baker-Miller pink (a pink color); Pakistan green (derived from green) with anti-flash white (from white colors); purple taupe (from grey) with mint (from green colors).

As a reminder, one of the ways the fashion industry pressures us women to buy new clothes more frequently is by not only changing the design, but also by introducing new "in-season" colors for almost every new season. They do this because colors are most noticed. They hope to make you feel uncomfortable wearing a different color than the "in" color. Avoid falling prey to this kind of a pressure. Some of the "in" colors may or may not fit you well. However, if you are somewhat sensitive to wearing these "in" colors, different shades of these colors may fit you better and solve the problem for you.

Chapter 8: Colors and Personal Style

The Subtle Impressions of Colors

Now that you generally understand which categories of colors best fit you, allow me to make a number of useful observations regarding specific colors and the image and/or subconscious impressions they may exude.

*B*lack is a color that looks good on everyone, but specially on "cool" people. It looks elegant and beautiful, and radiates more formality and "power." Black goes with practically every color so it makes it relatively easy to match different clothing items with it. However, if you wear predominantly black, you should be especially selective with accessories, shoes, jewelry and your hairstyle, making sure they all look more formal. Also, you need to take especially good care of black clothes to ensure they are clean and unwrinkled when you wear them. Although somewhat counter intuitive, wrinkles and dirt show more prominently, and attract more attention on black clothes, just as dust does on a shiny, black car.

*W*hite radiates purity, innocence and peace. This is why most wedding gowns are white. I am sure you will be surprised to hear me say that I don't recommend wearing much white. Although purity, innocence and peace are qualities everyone loves, white, in reality, is an "empty" color that evokes few emotions and catches little attention. This is not a color you want to wear if you want to look friendly or sexy. However, white, like black, does go well with all other colors. White also must be kept clean, as dirt will stand out prominently. "Warm" women look best in a soft or cream/ivory white color while "cool" women look fantastic in a milky white, as it has a slight bluish cast.

Orange is a very energetic color that catches a lot of attention. It evokes a sense of energy and vibrancy. However, be careful with this color as it is unusual and cannot be worn well by everyone. In reality, most women do not look good in orange, although it is a good color for those who do. Orange, of all shades, like yellow, looks best on "warm" people.

Blue is a very intriguing color that evokes mystique and quiet. As a result, subconsciously, it awakens our minds, which try to figure out and get a clearer reading of the person wearing this color. Softer shades of blue radiate logic, productivity, responsibly and self-control. This is why many business suits are shown in these shades. "Warm" types look fabulous in navy and Caribbean-water aqua, while "cool" types look best in sky blue and ice blue.

Red is an "aggressive" and attention-grabbing color which evokes a wide range of emotions. It is a "sexy" color as well as a color that emanates love. This is why red monopolizes Valentine's Day. People send red boxes of chocolate and red roses when they express love. On clothing, red looks better on women who are confident in themselves. Without a confidence, the color red will subconsciously

clash with the woman's personality. Red is great if you meet a man you like and are trying to attract. However, if you plan to meet a woman, think twice. Most likely you will come across as extremely aggressive and evoke her competitive instincts. For that same reason I wouldn't recommend wearing red at work, especially if your boss is a woman. Tomato red looks good on "warm" women, while red-blue looks best on "cool" ones.

*G*reen commonly appears in nature. It is a calming, relaxing color, but is otherwise pretty neutral in every other aspect. It is a "safe" color to wear for most occasions. For "warm" types I recommend green-lime or olive colors while, for "cool" types, I recommend a bluish-green, or a smoky-green.

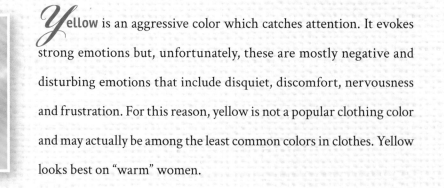

*Y*ellow is an aggressive color which catches attention. It evokes strong emotions but, unfortunately, these are mostly negative and disturbing emotions that include disquiet, discomfort, nervousness and frustration. For this reason, yellow is not a popular clothing color and may actually be among the least common colors in clothes. Yellow looks best on "warm" women.

*P*ink is a very difficult color, although a romantic and calming color. However, it doesn't look good on most people. Pink actually looks best on blond women who have light colored skin or on women with black hair. Since it works best as a contrast, it is a better choice of color for "warm" women.

*B*rown is the color of earth and is associated with natural and organic things. It suggests stability, reliability, approachability and a down-to-earth attitude. However, it is not an interesting color per se; rather, it is often perceived as a boring color since it generates few emotions other than calmness. I recommend caramel-brown for "warm" types and ice-brown for "cool" types.

*G*rey evokes two different emotions at the same time, positive and negative. On the one hand, it is calming, unthreatening and radiates simplicity, modesty, humility and obedience. For this reason it is a great color to wear at work around your boss. On the other hand, for historical reasons, it brings up a negative mindset outside of work. Grey is the color of ashes and has been associated with lifelessness throughout history; it also holds religious symbolism that is associated with punishment, repentance, fasting and prayer. I suspect that this is due to the fact that grey clothes were simple and cheap to produce. The dye, was simple and cheap to make, and could easily be applied to coarse, rough and unprocessed wool. As a result, grey became the color of the "commoners." However, grey clothing could appear more attractive if combined with nice fabric and non-simplistic, elegantly designed clothes. These clothes are great when you want to naturally exude power and richness, while you simultaneously want to come across as understated and modest. A strong grey will work best for "warm" types while a medium to light grey will be perfect for "cool" types.

*P*urple is a very complicated color. Purple embodies both the excitement and stimulation of the color red, while exuding the calmness of the color blue. This dichotomy may cause uneasiness unless its undertone is clearly defined as more of a red, or more of a blue, since at this point, the purple takes on the characteristics of its undertone. Purple evokes a sense of mystery as well as royal qualities,

and is often well-liked by very creative or eccentric people. Unfortunately, purple tends to make women look older. While this should pose no problem for younger women, a more mature woman should be more selective. A quiet purple is best worn by "warm" types while an aggressive purple should be worn by "cool" types.

Chapter 9

INTERPRETING YOUR BASIC WARDROBE

Clothes are an important element of how you project yourself to others. So far in this book, you learned about the importance of your personal style and how to appear stylish. It is now time to understand how to combine the different clothing elements in your wardrobe and use them to your ultimate advantage. The key operative word here is "**combine**." **How you project yourself at any given time depends on your complete outfit, not on any individual item.** Many women fall short in this area. In fact, in my opinion, few women do this well. Way too often, I see women ruin their overall looks because of a poor combination of clothes and colors. The individual items may have been fine, but their combination was bad. Worse yet, it amazes me how many women seem to believe that a single "fashionable" and/or "expensive" item is all that is required to project an image, so they pay only cursory attention to the rest of their clothes and accessories. We women are very quick to notice the "clueless" men who buy expensive jackets but wear plastic shoes, or wear expensive shoes with a polyester jacket, or wear items and/or colors that are completely mismatched.

Often, we laugh and joke among ourselves at how clueless these men are. How come we don't see these same errors in our own choices? True, we rarely make such obvious, screaming mistakes, but we do detract from the effectiveness of how we look by making smaller mistakes. Thus, my foremost rule about combining clothes is: It is never one single item but the entire outfit that counts! Of course,

87

great single items can add significantly to the overall look, but only if the rest of the combination works well with it to create an outfit. Unfortunately, combining clothes and colors is more of an art than a science. We need to understand what each individual item of clothing projects in order to understand how well the combination works. What follows are some basic observations regarding the different clothing categories. Also included are a reasonably exhaustive list and a short description of the many different styles under each category of clothing. Many of us are not completely familiar with all of the intricate names; becoming aware will help us better understand the implications of each when we read about them.

Basic Garments and the Effect of Combinations

In the following pages I offer broad observations regarding the different garment categories and specific items within each category. The purpose is to provide you with a basic understanding of what images are evoked by individual pieces and how to best combine them into stylish outfits.

I also discuss key accessories and how they can be used to enhance your look. Obviously, there are endless combinations that can be created; therefore I only provide general highlights and what I consider to be more relevant for the purpose of this book. Assume that these garments fit all body types unless otherwise indicated.

LOUSES

Blouses are very versatile and project a more formal, professional image than T-shirts do. You can wear a blouse with anything — pants, skirts or jeans. Eyes generally gravitate to the blouse, assuming you don't wear something loud as a bottom. Blouses also project a lot of power; even a boring suit becomes amazing with an interesting blouse. If you wear an outfit with a blouse, then the blouse should be the center of the outfit. Below are some finer observations regarding different blouses and the occasions where they might fit best.

Classic Business Suit blouses These blouses are very boring to me, but accomplish the objective of creating a basic business look. This kind of blouse is slim in shape and rarely comes in bright colors. Women at the beginning of their careers, professional women who provide consulting services to clients or women in the banking industry are wise to wear this kind of blouse as it projects a professional image. These blouses can be fun if you wear them with jeans for a more casual business image, a casual evening out, or after-work parties.

Button-front cotton blouses These are classic, basic blouses. Wear them with dress pants to appear more business-like, but since they are a bit loose the overall appearance is a little more on the informal side. Wear them with jeans to look classier for an informal, upscale image including a Sunday afternoon party. This type of blouse fits all body types well.

89

Ruffled blouses These blouses may have long sleeves, short sleeves or be sleeveless. They work well for small-chested women. They also project a very feminine look. Since the ruffles make the woman's top appear busy and complicated, the bottom part of her outfit should be plain and simple.

Empire waist blouses These blouses project a romantic, yet informal image. They are great to wear out on a date, as they look fancy and dressy. These blouses go well with pencil skirts, straight pants or any type of jeans. They also are useful for women who might want to camouflage a more pronounced stomach.

Ethnic blouses These blouses project an exotic, fun-loving image. They are feminine and romantic as well as always in fashion because they are perceived as vintage clothes.

Blouses with belts This kind of a blouse is usually belted and is not tucked in, but is worn outside of the bottom garment. Wearing a belt makes the blouse look more interesting, trendy and fashionable.

Button-fronted silk blouses A silk blouse that buttons in front is a basic wardrobe essential that projects simplicity and elegance at the same time. This kind of blouse serves as a great part of a fancier daily outfit. This blouse is all body types friendly, but is especially great for women with short torsos.

Shirred waist blouses A blouse with a shirred, or gathered waist is a great way to show off your waistline. This kind of a blouse fits most women nicely and rarely needs to be altered or taken in by a tailor.

Princess sleeve blouses These blouses have puffy shoulders. Whether the sleeves are short or long, this version of the garment projects a very feminine look perfect for cocktail parties. This blouse gives a more upscale image, in particular, when worn as part of a business outfit. It looks amazing on women with nice, skinny arms.

Cap-sleeved blouses This style of blouse has only the hint of a sleeve and covers only a small part of the arms. This style is great for summer dates and is especially good for women with bigger or fatter arms.

-SHIRTS

These are the most basic, yet very common kinds of tops. Comparatively inexpensive, you can own as many of them as you like and achieve different looks on a daily basis. They are especially well-suited to wear with jeans. I sometimes see women wearing T-shirts with simple-business pants; however, I don't recommend this as, to me, that combination looks a bit mismatched. I would also suggest you avoid wearing overly large, loose T-shirts. Wearing one of these may make you look like "one of the boys," but, more often than not, it gives the impression that you borrowed the shirt from a man. In either case, it never looks feminine! T-shirts are very versatile and can range in image from being simple and functional to being very sexy. But, always wear a size appropriate for you, or you risk losing the sexy image. You also may wear it under a jacket for a fancy, yet sporty look. Anyone can find a T-shirt in which they will look amazing.

T-shirts with pictures, signs and written messages We see these kinds of shirts everywhere and they are very acceptable. I believe that a nice, appealing picture or design pattern radiates a more upscale image and is fine to wear. This look is particularly appropriate for a night out dancing or to see a movie. However, if the shirt bears a sign, a humorous picture and/or a message of any kind, then be careful. Such shirts radiate an extremely casual image and detract from your overall attractiveness. They may be more appropriate to wear in settings where you feel very relaxed and don't care much about how attractive you come across.

SUMMER TOPS

These light tops can be very sexy and go well with pants, skirts and jeans. They can be worn with all colors, as long as the colors fit you and are part of a complete, coordinated outfit. Here are some examples of summer tops:

Square neckline tops These are very interesting and somewhat unusual. As such, they can be fun and offer an opportunity to wear something different. These tops look better on women with smaller breasts, but may work well for those with a larger bust, as well. Give it a try.

Sleeveless tops These are comfortable and fun! However you must be content with the appearance of your arms, as they will be more exposed. The sleeveless top is great for women with very feminine shoulders and arms!

Tank tops These generally are very boring but can be quite attractive if combined with other items and accessories, like jewelry or nicely tailored pants. You can choose your favorite colors and wear them perfectly with jeans during the day.

Animal print tops These tops are very popular any time. Since they are very colorful, fun and always catch a lot of attention, you should probably keep the rest of the outfit simple and subdued.

Gathered neckline tops These neckline tops are very interesting. They give an impression of vintage, yet appear chic at the same time. They offer a great outfit for a country club or other summer fun events.

One-shoulder tops These very sexy tops catch a lot of attention as they make the eyes pivot toward the bare shoulder, so make sure you, indeed, want to show that shoulder off.

Empire tops These tops have a high waistline that actually occurs just below the bosom. These tops are perfect for those who have a great bust but have a waistline that is not as complimentary as they would like. They look very romantic and can be worn with either jeans or other pants.

Tunic tops These tops always create a sophisticated look and go well with leggings or skinny jeans. They project a casual, yet stylish look.

Halter tops and A-line cut tops These are great for women with beautiful shoulders and nice arms. They are also especially good for women with large breasts, as they obscure your bust area.

Jacket and Blazers

Jackets and blazers are a must for all women! Jackets always project a more formal and upscale look. Black or darkly colored jackets offer more versatility and can be paired with pants, jeans, skirts, or even dresses of any color. Wear them with a blouse, a light sweater or even a nice T-shirt, but never with a heavy sweater. Pay specific attention to the length of the jacket, which should be appropriate for your height and the size of your torso. The shorter you are, the shorter your jacket should be. The style, shape and colors of some jackets could be difficult to pair with other pieces to create an outfit. I recommend you choose jackets which will work well with many different outfits. Here are a couple of observations regarding different styles of jackets

Classic blazers These jackets are mostly best worn for business. However, add a T-shirt and jeans to the mix and you'll have a completely different look. You can use the classic jacket for both, business and for going out socially, depending on what else you choose to wear with it.

Evening blazers These jackets generally project a more formal and upscale look. A hot red-colored jacket will always project a very fashionable look. You can wear this jacket with a casual or a formal dress, pants and even with jeans. Evening blazers are normally made from a different fabric that is more fun and could be shiny.

Colored blazers Pick your favorite color and have fun with it. Wear a colorful blazer with pants, skirts, jeans or dresses. This jacket will add a classy touch to any outfit. If you wear a brightly colored blazer, keep the rest of your outfit simple. Otherwise, the colors may clash and detract from your overall look.

Three-quarter sleeve blazers These jackets come with a single front button and always project a fresh, rich and luxurious look. They work well in almost any social setting and for any occasion, which means you always can wear this blazer with confidence. These jackets project both simplicity, and are fancy at the same time. Outfits combined with these jackets are particularly appropriate for visiting museums, galleries or participating in other unusual daytime events that require a look that is more chic.

Straight blazers These jackets are not fitted at the waist. As a result, they give a bit of a loose look. They look especially good when worn by women with bigger hips or wider waistlines because they hide the waist and hips, yet bring a great, balanced look between the lower and upper body.

$\mathcal{S}$WEATERS

You can find sweaters made from a variety of different materials from light-weight, fine, silky knits to very heavy, bulky wools. As a result, sweaters can be worn in the fall, winter and spring. They also go well with pants, jeans and skirts. When deciding on a sweater, you should first decide on the neck design that best fits you — a V-neck, crew or turtleneck. The color of the sweater is less important, as long as it is a color that suits you well. The material of the sweater, however, is important. The more refined the fiber, the more upscale the look.

Sweaters come in different styles and designs. They are very versatile and go well with everything, although I particularly like them worn with jeans. Like with T-shirts, I recommend you keep many sweaters of different styles and colors in your closet. This way, with only a few pairs of jeans, you can achieve a different look practically every day.

Below are some observations for your consideration regarding some sweater designs.

$\mathcal{B}$at-sleeved sweaters These generally appear more upscale and formal and offer a fresh, fancy and feminine look. They are particularly good for women whose waists are not well-defined or for those who are overweight.

$\mathcal{T}$urtleneck sweaters These sweaters are difficult to categorize. They look great on some women, but not on others. Be careful when you choose to wear this style, particularly if you have a short and/or a thick neck, this sweater will exaggerate that look.

Fancy sweaters These are the dressy sweaters that are nice to wear with jewelry, particularly necklaces. A nice, refined sweater with an open neck and proper jewelry will catch a lot of attention.

Simple sweaters Simple sweaters are not very flashy and don't catch much attention, however, they do elevate the overall look of an outfit. They look classy either with or without buttons and go well with jeans. They can look very sexy and can be used daily.

Striped sweaters These sweaters are always chic, however, if you plan to wear them, make sure everything else you wear is extremely simple.

Sweaters with princess sleeves These sweaters project a very feminine, informal and friendly look. They are particularly appropriate and flattering on women with narrow shoulders, as they make the shoulders appear wider.

Everyday V-neck sweaters These are very versatile and sexy sweaters that can be worn with either T-shirts, shirts or blouses — or can be worn alone with nothing underneath. I like to wear them with scarves.

Black sweaters These are very practical and look elegant regardless of whether they are embellished or simply worn alone. Since black goes well with almost anything, this color offers you a wide variety of options for outfit combinations. You can wear black sweaters everywhere — in the office; for a short walk; while shopping; or while at a café or restaurant. They are classic and look great on every body type.

Thin sweaters These sweaters are made of fine, light-weight fibers. I like to wear them routinely and when on vacation. They can be worn in different colors and with different neckline shapes. Sleeve lengths also can vary — long, three-quarters, elbow-length or short. These sweaters are very comfortable and look great; however they require you to make sure that they don't look old or dirty. Fancy sweaters can be used with fancy pants for a special, upscale and chic look.

CARDIGANS

Cardigan sweaters are made from either wool, cotton or silk and open in the front. They are very useful as you can wear them with almost everything, despite the style, including jeans, pants, skirts, daytime dresses and evening dresses. Generally, these sweaters are not costly; therefore, you can buy them in multiple colors and use them frequently.

Fancy cardigans These look dressy and catch attention. They provide a fancier look and go best with a skirt, making a great outfit for an evening at a restaurant.

Cardigans with collars These sweaters give you a look of wearing a jacket; therefore, you should always wear something underneath it. Although nice looking, they rarely appear fancy or formal, as their design is generally more relaxed and homey.

Classic cardigans These have a simple design with little embellishment or stylish details. They usually button-down, and are knit with either a V-neck or round neck. Although simple, they do look interesting and go well with practically everything. They look good in almost every color and offer great functionality, particularly whenever you need something that will keep you warm when chilly.

Long cardigans These items are great to complete an outfit, but do look better with pants or jeans, rather than with skirts or dresses.

ℙANTS

Pants are very versatile and a "must have" for every women. You can wear them everywhere, whether it is to work, for a walk, to visit friends or to a party. You can have pants in many different colors, although the most versatile and functional colors are black or darker colors. Dark-colored pants are the easiest to combine with blouses, sweaters, tops or jackets. You can achieve a casual look by wearing a nice pair of pants with a casual shirt, a blouse or a jacket. You can create a fancier, more formal look if you match your pants with more formal-looking tops. If the pants are a soft, quite color, it is best to match them with a stronger, louder colored top, and vice-versa; with aggressively colored pants, your top should contain quiet colors. Shoes with high heels help enhance the overall appeal of pants.

Tailored pants These pants offer a nice, business-like look. They are simple and basic, yet classic, and should be in every closet. They look good on everyone and provide quite a sophisticated look.

Cotton pants These are extremely casual beach-pants. They are very useful for daily wear and can be of any color and worn with sport, flats or platform shoes.

Wide-legged pants Pants with wide legs are generally roomy and provide a sense of comfort, particularly during the summer months. These are a very good choice for women who may be a bit "bow-legged."

*traight-legged pants* These are the pants that do not taper towards the bottom, but have an even width throughout the leg. They are popular, look nice and are very comfortable. These pants are very complimentary for most women and can be used informally during daily routines as well as at work.

kinny pants These pants have a complicated look and are not for everybody. They will emphasize leg shapes and also tend to make the lower part of your legs appear larger, so be cautious if you decide to choose to wear them.

Jeans are probably the most popular of all pants. Over the past ten to fifteen years, jeans have migrated from being simple and very casual in both material and design into creating a fancy and high-fashion look. No woman should be without them. Buy as many pairs as you wish and can afford in different styles so you could change your image daily. You may wear jeans with shirts, T-shirts, blouses, jackets, sweaters or tops. Fancy jeans will always look nice, but will look even fancier with high-heeled shoes. Casual jeans look better with flats or nice sneakers. Jeans come in many shapes, styles and designs, so be sure to buy only the ones that compliment your body type well — the ones that accent the positive and cover the negatives. Below you will find some useful observations regarding different jean designs.

109

*C*ropped jeans These pants are very risky as they can easily be worn incorrectly. This style can make your legs look shorter; therefore, if you have short legs, these might not be for you. This style can also make your middle look wider, so, if you wear them, choose the correct top to avoid drawing attention to your hips. These pants do look better with high heels, but, to create a more casual look, wear flats. Make sure your legs are long enough to look good in this style.

Skinny jeans These jeans fit tightly around the legs. This cut makes a woman's legs look longer and, therefore, make them look very sexy. You must be cautious, however, as these jeans are more appropriate for skinnier women with nicely shaped legs. If you are not sure about how your legs look to others, you may be better off with another style, as this one will quickly show all your flaws.

Straight-legged jeans These are jeans that are cut straight from the hips down to the bottom of the legs. They give you a classic jeans look, go well with all body types and are appropriate for most occasions. For these reasons, they are very popular and likely to stay popular for a long time. Every woman should have this style on hand. Combine these jeans with a T-shirt for a simple, sporty look, or with a blouse or sweater for a fancier look. They also can be worn with a jacket for a more formal look, which also works well even at work.

Flared jeans These are the jeans that become wider from the knees down. They provide a bit of an old-fashioned look and style. Very popular in 1970s and '80s, they are beginning to experience a resurgence. Be careful, however, as these jeans project a heavier appearance that makes the legs appear to be a little shorter. Therefore, if you are short or have disproportionately short legs, you might want to avoid this style. Also, they are probably more appropriate for informal occasions.

Boot cut jeans These pants have a cut very similar to straight jeans but are wider at the ankles. They provide a classic jeans look that go well with most body types. This style is my favorite as its cut tends to create an impression of a balanced body shape. They are especially good for women with a wider waistline, as this cut draws attention away from the waist and onto your legs. They offer a wonderful sporty look, and are appropriate for all sporting events or other fun activities.

SHORTS

Obviously, shorts are great for summer wear. Shorts are very comfortable, allow freedom of movement and can look chic to boot. Shorts project a predominately casual look; however, those with attractive designs combined with a fancy top will project a more upscale look. Shorts can look great as part of a sporty outfit and become very functional as a beach outfit. Although their comfort is very tempting, particularly on a hot summer day, shorts are not appropriate for everyone. They are best worn by women with nice legs and good figures. They may not necessarily be complimentary on others.

Hot pants These are the fancy designer shorts that are generally shorter and more revealing. They can look fashionable and very sexy, but only for those who feel they have a nice figure and nice legs. Avoid these if you don't have a befitting figure and legs. It is especially wise to avoid these if your buttocks are heavy, as the heavier they are, the more you are at risk for being perceived as "cheap" or even "vulgar." This look is not appropriate for women who are older. However, if you are young and have nice legs, then be my guest and wear them. Hot shorts look great with high-heeled shoes.

Long shorts (Bermuda shorts, Capri pants) These are knee, or just over-the-knee-length shorts and are generally comfortable, as they are not too tight nor too wide. For that reason, they look cute on practically everybody. They also are appropriate for all ages and are great to wear on vacation and on the beach.

Cotton sport shorts Stylish and very comfortable, these shorts are appropriate not just for sporty activities, but also offer a cute, casual look during the summer, by a swimming pool or at the beach.

UITS

Suits can be divided into conservative versus less conservative, and fancy versus daily. Dark color suits normally are better to wear during the winter, while lighter colors are best to wear during the summer.

Skirt suits These suits always look feminine and very sexy, particularly when worn by women with nice legs. They generally project a more conservative look; however, a fun, dressy, fancy skirt can convert this into a cute, flirty outfit.

Business pantsuits These usually are simple in design without a lot of detail. Their straight, classic cut pants make the legs appear longer. Pantsuits project a more formal, business-like look. Every woman should have one, particularly, if you frequently mingle with business people. This way, you will not feel awkward or out of place around them, whether men or women. These suits are appropriate for many occasions, but specifically where a more formal or professional look is desired. This style makes it easy to look groomed and pulled together and as a result you will be taken more seriously.

Tailored cotton suits These are very light and comfortable; for this reason, they are great to wear during the summer. They are very popular and project a casual, relaxed appearance. These suits look good in most colors as long as the colors flatter you. However, lighter colors are more appropriate and look better when worn during summer months.

SKIRTS

Skirts are a woman's blessing as they make any woman look more feminine and always catch men's attention. However, make sure you wear a design that fits your body type. Obviously, skirts completely reveal your legs and will draw attention to them.

Someone once said that if you possess fewer clothes in some categories, then you don't care for that part of your body. I believe this to be true. I don't like my legs so I don't own many skirts. If you are a woman who is lucky to have nice legs, then skirts are your chance to show them off!

Pencil skirts These skirts work very well with any body type except for those who have wider hips. These look nice when worn with a blouse, a blouse plus a jacket, or sweaters but are more effective when worn as part of a business outfit. By adding a bright top and accessories, you can make it more fun and fancy. These skirts are classic and sexy at the same time. Depending on what you wear as a top you can achieve different looks. With a classic shirt and jacket, your look will be more professional and more appropriate in the office, while a fancy blouse will give you a more fun look and is very appropriate for going out socially.

Pencil skirt with ruffles This kind of skirt is mostly formal, but the ruffles give them a feminine and flirty look. This skirt style also makes it easy to achieve different looks, depending on what you wear with them.

Tiered skirts These skirts are informal and feminine because they have a lot of ruffles and offer you a bit of a youthful look. This type of skirt is ideal to wear on a vacation or to go out dancing since it exudes a fun look.

Bubble skirts These are drum-shaped — narrow at the top and bottom, but wide in the middle. Usually, these skirts go well with any body type, but are particularly appropriate for women with both larger or smaller hips. If your hips are larger, this style will cover them; if your hips are smaller (boyish), this style will make them appear fuller. These skirts generally look better when they are made from a firmer fabric, as the harder fabric maintains the shape of the skirt better. However, bubble, puffball skirts have a tendency to make you look heavier, so you might want to use a fitted rather than a puffy top to avoid looking too voluminous everywhere.

A-line skirts These skirts are appropriate for all body types, but the length of the skirt is important and needs to be considered. For example, if your bottom is heavier, the skirt should fall to below the knee. These skirts are really easy to wear and look especially cute with blouses, short blazers or jackets. They do, however, tend to draw attention to the waist.

DRESSES

The most classic and most important item of women's clothing, dresses have defined womanhood and femininity since the beginning of time and radiate an immediate impression of femininity. The greatest thing about dresses is that they come in a variety of styles, shapes and colors and any woman can find the perfect dress for her body type and for any occasion.

All nice clothes make women feel good, but dresses stand out in a category of their own. These are the only garments that actually may alter our psychology and inner feelings. When we put on any nice garment we tend to believe we look good and, therefore, we become more proud and confident. However, putting on a pretty dress creates a whole different transformation. Wearing the appropriate dress for the right occasion is a "ritual" for a women and a "spiritual experience."

Our mood changes as soon as we begin to put on a dress; we can't wait to see ourselves in it. In other words, we personally very much enjoy the process of putting on a pretty dress; if we like the result, our confidence level instantly shoots up. Dresses make us look feminine. I love dresses and love to prepare to go out in a dress I think will give me the look I want.

Therefore, go ahead and indulge! It is impossible to own too many dresses! Dresses come in all types and shapes and are extremely versatile. They can go well with sandals or shoes in the summer and with boots in the winter. However, just be sure to select the dress that compliments your body type. Here are some observations regarding some dress styles.

Dresses with wide belts These dresses are very eye-catching and different; as such, they are best worn for special occasions rather than for daily wear. They work best for special events like cocktail events, fundraisers and store opening events. Their wide belts tend to make your waist look narrower.

Strapless dresses These are mostly summer dresses and are great for the beach and for vacations. They are simple to wear, put on and take off and have an easy-going, comfortable look that actually makes you feel light and relaxed. These dresses look good with most colors and in most lengths. They also may be worn with or without a strap.

A-line skirt-dresses These dresses are especially good for women with larger hips, and/or boyish figures as they obscure the shape of the hips.

Skirt and blouse dresses These dresses look more like skirts and blouses rather than like a single dress. They are a fun choice and, depending on what you plan to wear with it, can be worn for a business-casual look or as a weekend night out outfit.

Maxi-dresses These dresses always look fashionable, yet are very comfortable. They are romantic and look casual, yet chic; therefore, can be worn daily even while on vacation, or anywhere else you want to feel more at ease and comfortable. You can wear them around town, at the beach or at the swimming pool.

Wrap dresses These dresses are very versatile. They look good on most body types and are appropriate for all age groups, but are more fitting for summer wear. You can wear them on a daily basis whether you are working in the office or going for coffee. Pair them with nice jewelry to create a fun, "party" look.

COCKTAIL DRESSES

These dresses, which offer a more formal and stylish look, come in many different styles and colors. Any woman can find a cocktail dress that will flatter her body. However, please avoid one very common mistake I see happen over and over again. Many women, due to the influence of the fashion industry, believe that sleeveless cocktail dresses and formal gowns that reveal the neck, back and shoulders are the nicest. Indeed, for the right woman, this style will prove very complimentary and sexy, so go for it! However, please remember to choose clothes appropriate for **your** body type — first and foremost. Again, don't just buy what the fashion industry tries to sell you. Avoid sleeveless cocktail dresses if you have larger arms and bigger shoulders. Such dresses will only make them appear more pronounced. Instead, choose dresses that have short sleeves and cover your shoulders, partly or fully; otherwise, you might want to add a nice shawl to cover your shoulders and upper arms.

How about color? Renowned fashion designer Coco Chanel once said that every woman should have a little black dress. Indeed, blackish colors with more formal and stylish designs always look classy and elegant as long as their designs are not overcomplicated. In other words, black cocktail dresses are always safe and can be worn everywhere for all occasions, regardless of how casual or formal the occasion may be. Moreover, a black cocktail dress has the additional benefit of being especially flattering on women who wish to appear slimmer. I highly recommend that each woman own at least one black cocktail dress with a simple, elegant design that best fits her body type. However, the dresses that catch the most attention and enhance a woman's looks most measurably are dresses with color. Some specific observations regarding some of the more common categories of cocktail dresses follow.

Strapless, no-waist dresses These dresses draw attention to the shoulders and décolleté. Therefore, please be careful, as these may be more appropriate for women with better figures.

Ladies dresses These are feminine, elegant and classic, appropriate anywhere, for any occasion where a cocktail dress is needed.

Dresses without a waistline These dresses are more appropriate for a business occasion, but can double as a cocktail dress. If you choose stronger colors, this dress will project a fun look as an evening outfit.

121

Formal knee-length and tea-length dresses These have become very popular in recent years. Knee-length dresses generally end at about the knees, while tea-length dresses are a bit longer and end somewhere between the knees and the upper part of the calf. Both types differ from regular cocktail dresses as they are fancier and have more complicated and sophisticated designs. This style is appropriate for any occasion that requires a cocktail dress and may even serve as a great replacement for an actual formal evening gown.

Pencil dresses These dresses offer the advantage of being appropriate for both daytime business occasions as well as for after-hours cocktail events. They are classic outfits and if you are unsure which clothes to wear for a particular event, the pencil dress will most likely fit the occasion. I believe that every woman should have at least one in her closet.

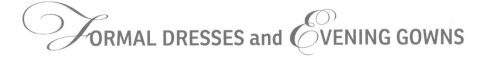

FORMAL DRESSES and EVENING GOWNS

These long dresses are normally made of luxurious fabrics and, as such, radiate a very formal and elegant look. Depending on which style you select, you can achieve practically any image you would like ranging from quiet and elegant, to stunning and sexy. This dress category comes in many designs and styles. Some designs incorporate sewn-in glittery and shiny items. Personally, I prefer this type because these enhancements make these dresses look fancier and more eye-catching. However, the glitter of the dress must be in balance with the jewelry you may wear.

You may wear as much jewelry as you like as long as there isn't too much glitter or shine on the dress itself. If a lot of glitter and shine appears on the dress, then wear less jewelry. These dresses come in all price ranges, so most women can find at least one that fits their price range and style preference. I recommend wearing lighter colors in the summer, including flowery dresses with a mixture of colors, or multi-colored dresses, depending on your tastes. It is best to wear single-colored, darker-toned dresses during the winter. Here, too, please be aware of your body type, particularly if you choose to wear a dress designed to reveal your upper body. If you have beautiful shoulders and arms, then you need not worry; otherwise, be careful and select your choices wisely.

COATS

Coats are a very important part of colder climate wardrobes. We wear these garments more frequently than any other single clothing item during the spring, autumn and winter months. As they are the outermost layer we wear, coats are the first clothing items people notice — and we all know the value of a "first impression."

Unfortunately, coats are generally expensive; they can be much more so than any other clothing item. As such, most can't afford to buy several of them. As a result, great care should be given to the coats we do purchase to ensure they provide a great degree of versatility while they complement our looks as we wear many different outfits. At a minimum, I would recommend women have two coats if they live in areas of warm or mild weather, and four coats if they live in areas where winters are cold. The two for cold weather should be heavier while the spring and autumn wear should be lighter.

Two of these coats should be multi-purpose for daily, more frequent use, while the others should be appropriate for more formal evenings and special occasions. Like dresses, coats come in many designs, colors and "flavors." One can go crazy trying to determine which looks nicest on us. Don't. Instead, I suggest you select a coat that reflects your personal style as well as the first impression that you wish to create with people. Below are some observations regarding various coat designs.

Wrap coats These coats do not have buttons or zippers but are normally held closed by belts. They project a fancier, more sophisticated look, but generally are not warm enough for really cold weather. These coats fit most body types so, if you like the way they look on you, feel free to wear one.

Toggle coats These coats are predominately informal, simple and always in style. They go well with most body types, fit many different styles and look good no matter the age of the woman wearing them. A classic style, they are great for daily use.

*D*ouble-breasted *coats* These coats are classic and stylish. They radiate an elegant, feminine look and may be appropriate for either business or for a night out.

*A*ctive coats These are generally sporty in style and are a bit looser to provide comfort and a freedom of movement. They normally come with front zippers and radiate an informal, but stylish look. If you use diamond-quilted designs, you'll achieve a more classic style.

*S*hort coats with belts These are very interesting coats. The belt is the most important element of this coat, which generally portrays a more casual, simpler look.

Fur Coats

Fur coats are generally the most coveted by women, assuming, of course, they bear no conscientious objections to wearing animal fur. These coats tend to be more expensive but do exude a very special, luxurious look. Who can resist touching one? Aside from looking luxurious, they are also quite functional since they are lightweight and will keep you warm even in the coldest weather. Although very luxurious, they easily can also be used daily. Fur coat designs are generally divided into two types — the more traditional and classic designs, which have been with us for a long time and seem never to go out of style, and the more recent "fun" designs. Generally, the more traditional and classic designs will fit any age group, while the more fun designs are better worn by those who are younger.

Two overall dimensions differentiate fur coats: (a) the animal from which the fur is taken, as different animal furs represent a wide array of luxury looks and feels, their weights and the way they retain their initial luxurious look and feel over time; and (b) whether the coat is made from "whole-body" animal furs, or different "pieces" sewn together to create one coat.

Pieces, in this context, generally refer to fur straps of less than 14 inches long sewn together. Whether the coat is from pieces or is whole-body directly correlates with the look, durability and the cost of the fur coat. Generally, a fur that is more luxurious, lighter weight and retains its texture and shine longer over time will be more expensive. At the same time, "whole-body" furs are more durable since pieced fur coats include many more seams; this will make them less durable as the more seams present a greater vulnerability to wear and tear and literally may come apart more easily. Additionally, the overall shine and luster of coats created from fur pieces degrade faster over time than those made from whole body furs. For these reasons, as you may suspect, the cost of "piece-made" coats is substantially less and, therefore, are more affordable than the whole-body versions.

Cut fur coats This style refers to the normally long-hair fur cut to a shorter length. The longer hair augments the natural shine of the fur, making it appear more luxurious and eye-catching. The shorter hair softens this natural shine, creating a quieter, subdued, elegant and vintage look.

A-line fur coats These coats offer a very nice look. This style is great for overweight women since this style effectively covers the places where we don't want to attract attention. However, these coats are less practical during cold winter weather months, particularly when frequent winds blow, as the open design allows the wind to penetrate under the coat.

Knee-length fur coats These coats are very practical and can be used both daily, in the work environment as well as for social occasions. Their look is a bit simpler, but they radiate an elegant, warm and classy image.

Short chinchilla fur coats These beautiful furs attract a lot of attention. They radiate a very fancy appearance, which makes them more appropriate for more formal, upscale events, however, are not very practical. Although this fur is very soft, nice and sexy to the touch, it is very delicate and prone to damage. These furs also do not maintain warmth as well in the winter. If you wear one of these coats, plan to carry a small purse as an accessory — the smaller the better, as a larger purse is not a good pairing with the delicate, eye-catching look of a chinchilla.

*L*EATHER COATS

These coats look attractive and are both very practical and durable, especially in windy places. They are best worn during the spring and fall. Black, the most popular color for these coats, is the safest choice. Although they come in a variety of designs, the classic ones provide a more conventional, yet distinctive look and, therefore, are the safest choice.

*L*onger vs. shorter leather coats Longer coats are warmer in the winter, even though they are generally not as attractive as the shorter ones. The longer coats project a rougher look, while the shorter ones appear more attractive, stylish, elegant and classy. Also, shorter coats go better with less formal, sporty clothes. An older, more mature woman may want to consider wearing a belt with the coat, as this highlights the waistline and exudes a more elegant look.

132

$\mathscr{S}$CARVES and $\mathscr{S}$HAWLS

Scarves and shawls are wonderful accessories that can enhance your appearance. When used well, these items can create a fresh and fancy addition like pieces of jewelry. Use them properly and they will help you attract positive attention; however, be certain not to overdo it as, if you do, you may achieve a negative outcome. Using scarves and shawls can help you create "different" outfits and looks, which can prove quite a cost savings! However, to achieve the appearance of "different" looks, scarves need to contain colors different than those in your tops. Otherwise, although they will add to your look, they will be perceived as just part of your outfit rather than generating a "different" look.

Scarves can be worn around the neck or over one's shoulders. Although traditionally considered winter accessories, with the advent of new and lighter materials, we can now enjoy scarves during the summer as well. Summer scarves and shawls actually can prove very useful during the hot summer, as they can provide you some cover and relief when you retreat inside to cold, heavily air-conditioned rooms.

Hats

Hats also can be an interesting and a fashionable accessory. Aside from being able to use a hat to cover up messy hair, hats are effective in adding to your look; like scarves, they provide the illusion of a completely different outfit. Below are some observations with regards to wearing hats. Please note that there is an art to being able to wear a hat well; you need to know how to wear them, when they are appropriate and which ones are best for you. Choose the style of a hat you like but also make sure it goes well with the shape and skin color of your face.

Formal-looking hats These go well only with more formal outfits and only should be worn for more formal or fancy events. Otherwise, they look too pretentious and out of place, which will make you look silly, particularly in the U.S. where they are not very common. Keep in mind that these hats are large and fancy-looking, which means they will catch a lot of attention at the expense of people noticing the rest of your outfit. More often than not, these hats are statement-making accessories. However, please remember, when trying to make a statement, bigger does not necessarily mean better. Consider the possibility of more subtle ways you can use instead of a hat to make a statement.

Baseball caps These work well and look sexy, especially when worn with jeans, T-shirts and sneakers or boots. These caps are best worn while involved with outdoor activities rather than for formal or fancy events.

Cowboy hats These hats are terrific when worn in traditionally "cowboy" states, but look out of place in the Midwest and in northern states. At times, they offer an interesting and attractive look, however, more often than not, they appear strange to people in other geographic areas where they are not normally worn. My advice is to avoid wearing them unless you plan to spend an evening square dancing.

Fedoras Formerly considered a man's hat, times have changed; women now wear fedoras quite a bit as well. These work well when worn with jeans and T-shirt or with a summer beach dress.

Knit caps These used to be mostly a winter accessory for young girls, but now have found their way into mainstream fashion and are considered acceptable. Normally sold as part of a set along with scarves and gloves, these caps actually offer a great way to add lovely colors to the dreary, colorless winter months. They are very appropriate and look great with informal outfits, so feel free to enjoy them.

Fur hats These hats come in a variety of shapes and designs and are very attractive, although not terribly appropriate in informal settings. Therefore, they should be confined to winter wear. Choose a hat to match the coat you are wearing and you will appear VERY stylish!

Hats for church-weddings These can be very elegant and fashionable, but only are appropriate for special occasions and for those who wish to make a statement or look more classically fashionable. They are not all that common in the U.S., so you may run a risk of appearing pretentious and egocentric.

Baker boy caps These have become strangely very fashionable nowadays, but may be just a fad. Be cautious if you enjoy wearing these, as they look good on some women, but not on all.

Berets These are very "French" in appearance and are actually very feminine. They work well with more formal, classic outfits but don't work as well when worn with informal, casual wear, as they seem out of place in the U.S.

137

Shoes

Here is an interesting phenomenon. Until about 20 years ago, shoes were merely a utility item; women had very few pairs in their possession. Over the past decade, however, shoes have graduated to become an item of art and an important part of any outfit. Women today cannot seem to have enough shoes! Often, I think women like their shoes more than their jewelry. Shoes come in all shapes, colors and designs, as well as in a variety of price ranges. Go ahead and indulge! The renowned French footwear designer Christian Loboutin said it best, "Shoes keep a woman, but not the opposite!"

However, be careful when it comes to shoes. They seem to be nicer and more appealing to us when they are smaller in size and narrower in design. We, therefore, tend to gravitate toward buying smaller, tighter shoes. This is a huge mistake! The shoes may look nicer, but, over the years, they will likely ruin your foot health and, sometimes, even foot appearance. I have many friends who fell prey to this trap and now are paying the price for it. My conclusion is that it is not worth it! Therefore, find shoes that fit you well, that are very comfortable and that you can walk in comfortably, even if they are a bit more costly. Also, because the design and color selections are endless, buy only what appeals most to you.

UNGLASSES

Fantastic accessories, sunglasses are my favorite as they can actually completely change your appearance. I like to wear big sunglasses. Unlike other parts of your clothing and accessories, sunglasses are among the few items where displaying a designer's logo prominently does not detract from your looks or make you appear too pretentious. Needless to say, sunglasses are most handy at those times when we have no opportunity to work on our makeup; at these times, the larger the frame, the better the cover-up! There is also nothing like a pair of sunglasses to provide you with a different appearance instantly. Sunglasses come in many shapes and colors, as well as a price ranges. Since most are fairly affordable, I recommend you own as many as you like, however, make sure they go well with the shape of your face. Here are some observations about my favorite shapes and designs.

Oversized sunglasses Oversized sunglasses are very popular among Hollywood personalities and other celebrities. The preference for larger-frame sunglasses began with Jacqueline Bouvier Kennedy Onassis (better known as "Jackie O.") and actress Audrey Hepburn; they now are more commonly used. These glasses radiate a fun, chic image and go best with dressy outfits. These larger glasses look better on larger faces and look unattractive — and almost funny, on those with smaller faces.

Aviator sunglasses These glasses are best known as being replicas of those worn by military pilots. These glasses fit many face shapes and portray a more classic, pragmatic, serious, no-nonsense demeanor.

Unisex sunglasses Personally, I like the Unisex style and find them very versatile. They portray a more upscale yet "devilish" image and go well with business, fancy and sporty outfits. They tend to look better on round faces.

142

Wrap sunglasses These glasses are not very versatile. If you like them, make sure they go well with the shape of your face. They are not attention grabbers but do portray an image of pragmatism. They work great to protect eyes from sunrays, as they shield the eyes from the sides, not just from the front.

Wayfarer sunglasses These glasses represent a classic style that never goes out of fashion. They portray a more upscale, yet mysterious image. Be cautious, however, as they do not look good on some face shapes.

$\mathcal{B}$AG

Now, what can we say about handbags? Handbags were the "trail blazers" for a new trend in the fashion industry, turning what used to be simple, functional accessories, into fashion statements by themselves. They became so popular and successful that the fashion industry started to promote shoes, sunglasses and jewelry in the same way. However, handbags still remain in a class of their own.

Over the last 30 years, handbags transformed from just boring and burdensome accessories to items women love to carry and show off. We can't have enough of them and the market abides; it helps provide us with bags of seemingly endless shapes, designs and sizes, including casual, formal and anything in-between bags — enough to fit any woman's taste for any occasion. The proper handbag is now an absolute necessity to complete any outfit, however the bag must go well with the outfit with which it is paired, particularly when it is for a more upscale or formal event. A proper bag is important, as you may ruin the whole look of your outfit with a bag that does not match.

I love bags and cannot own enough of them. However, some can be costly, so choose wisely. Following are some observations regarding bags.

143

*T*ypes of Handbags

I like to separate my bags into two groups — the bags I use most regularly and those that are more upscale, which I use for more special occasions. As an overriding rule, I suggest that the handbag is probably the item most critical to complete your outfit — but on the **downside, not on the upside!** This means that no matter how beautiful or expensive the bag may be, it never defines your overall look; the outfit you wear does this! But, a poorly matched bag will significantly detract from your overall look, regardless of how well you may dress otherwise. More simply stated, **a handbag will rarely add to the image your clothes create, but can surely ruin the look of an otherwise great image.**

How to Choose the Appropriate Bag

There are three aspects that can act as spoilers if the bag is not chosen well: **color**, **size** and **style.**

Color

The greatest spoiler is a color that does not match the rest of your outfit. The bag may or may not be the same color as your outfit, but must match and be well-coordinated with the colors in your outfit; if not, the clashing contrast will scream at people and make you appear to be fashion- and style-blind.

Size

The bag's size must be appropriate for the outfit and occasion. Generally, the larger bags go better with daily and sporty outfits, while the smaller sizes go better with more formal and elegant outfits. For very formal occasions and a formal dress the most appropriate size is a small one.

Style

The style of the handbag must be consistent with the image of your outfit. If you wear a formal outfit, your bag should look more formal; if you wear an upscale outfit, your bag should look more fancy and upscale; if you wear an informal outfit, your bag should look informal as well. There are three things regarding bags that you should keep in mind:

- If your outfit appears to be expensive, do not use an obviously inexpensive bag, since it will cheapen your overall look.

- Bags that have lost their original shape, look beaten up or well-used, or are noticeably damaged are major negatives, no matter how expensive and prestigious they originally may have been.

- A high quality knock-off could work fine, however, avoid cheap designer bag replicas. Sometimes, the good quality knock-offs are done well and are difficult to distinguish from real ones, but the cheap replicas are obvious to everyone and will make you appear cheap and "fake."

$\mathcal{B}$elow are some basic observations of the more typical bag styles, which are my favorites.

$\mathcal{U}$nusual bags These bags generally contain a modern design with some catchy features. They are unusual and definitely attract attention, as they appear glamorous, hot, sexy and beautiful in design. The major drawback of these bags, however, is that most are really part of a fad and may quickly fall out of fashion. I like them because they are a great way to draw attention and appear different. They go better with more formal outfits and are best used in more formal situations.

$\mathcal{S}$atchels These bags display flat bottoms and two handles. A woman with a satchel bag tends to appear older, more mature and more serious. These bags, which range in size from medium to large, are more practical and functional.

$\mathcal{Z}$ip-top totes These bags, which are actually tote bags with a zipper at the top, usually come in larger sizes, but you can find them in smaller sizes as well. The larger sizes are more informal in appearance and go best with casual outfits like jeans and shorts.

   Some of the smaller designs may look sharper, more attractive and appear to be of better quality; these can be used with any style outfit. As a general rule, the more formal the outfit you wear, the smaller and more formal the handbag should be. You may use any size, shape or color bag with casual attire.

Leather bags Basic, attractive and versatile accessories that work well for a variety of occasions, leather bags are very practical and functional, making them ideal for everyday use. They are a good investment because leather is durable and the bag will serve you well for a long time.

Handbags These are short-handled bags that must always be hand-held. This can prove to be a real disadvantage; in fact, they can sometimes be a pain to deal with, as one of your hands is always occupied. The sporty look is more appropriate to use with casual outfits, while the more upscale and formal look is appropriate to use with more formal attire.

Embellished evening bags These smaller, more formal handbags are often embellished with crystals or jewelry for decoration. Elegant and lovely-looking, they frequently attract positive attention. As they are definitely fancy, they should be worn only with more upscale, formal outfits.

Clutches These are medium-sized bags and are considered in a category between the embellished and the smaller, formal evening bags. As they are medium-sized, they are a bit more functional than the smaller, formal evening bags and are appropriate in both formal and slightly more casual situations. However, although they definitely work well for both, they are not as "formal" and "glamorous"-looking as the smaller, formal evening bags.

Tote bag Totes are normally long and may or may not also have a zipper at the top. They look elegant and very functional, especially for travel or for the beach.

Exotic skin bags These very special and always attractive bags are made of real, exotic leather. As they are very elegant and upscale, they radiate a more mature and sophisticated image. I suggest young women avoid accessorizing with these bags.

Evening bags These are the smallest, most formal handbags which are only appropriate for more formal occasions. Beautiful in design, they exude an extremely elegant image and definitely attract attention due to their beauty. However, on the downside, they are often too small to have any functionality and frequently can be quite expensive.

Evening satin bags These satin bags top the list for being elegant, fancy, beautiful, feminine and always fashionable. Typically, they are more suitable for formal occasions.

Hobo bags Usually made from a soft or flexible material like fabric or leather, these bags come in larger sizes and have only a single strap. They radiate a more casual appearance, yet are very stylish at the same time. They look best when used with a summer dress or jeans. Movie stars love them.

Shoulder bags These bags are normally informal but offer a huge advantage. Since they are carried on your shoulder, your hands are free. Therefore, these bags are perfect for situations where you may need both hands, like when shopping.

Patent leather bags These shiny bags look luxurious and are very stylish.

$\mathcal{B}$ELTS

Belts may be small in size but require extra care for use. For the most part, they may have a neutral effect on your look, but a well-selected belt can provide a major appearance enhancement. Unfortunately, like the bag, a poorly selected belt can greatly detract from your overall outfit.

$\mathcal{B}$lack leather belts These leather belts grab attention. Although generally glamorous, they may appear busy, so they will go best with a simpler outfit.

$\mathcal{L}$arge, jeweled buckle belts Classic belts, particularly those with simple metal buckles, are good for most occasions, especially when worn with jeans and pants.

$\mathcal{N}$arrow belts These narrow belts are very common and simple, but are elegant and are great when worn to show off your waist, if that feature is something you are proud of. They work particularly well with dresses and skirts.

$\mathcal{F}$abric belts Informal, but very feminine and rather romantic, fabric belts go well with both dresses and skirts.

$\mathcal{W}$ide belts As they make an outfit and the person wearing it look somewhat "heavy" and bulky, wide belts are more appropriate for thinner women. However, they do attract attention and look especially good when worn on your hips and when worn with simpler, lighter outfits.

Chapter 10

ORGANIZING YOUR CLOTHES

We talked about the fact that the best clothes you own are those you have collected over time and use again and again over many years. However, unless you take good care of those clothes, they are not likely to last and continue to look good. How you store your clothes in your closet helps determine how fresh they look and how long they last. I, for one, love my closet. My clothes are my treasure and my closet is my treasure chest. I believe that if a man's home is his castle, a woman's castle is her closet. Therefore, let's review how you can best organize and maintain a functional closet. This review will provide you with an opportunity to peek into mine, which will make what I tell you more real for you.

153

Closet Organization

From what I have seen, most closets are poorly organized. This is true regardless of whether the closet is small or is a large, walk-in one. Often, I arrived at my friends' homes as they tried to decide what to wear. Even though each was very excited about going out for the evening, the journey of getting dressed was far from pleasurable; instead, the process made them anxious and became a nerve wracking experience. When they couldn't find specific items they were looking for, both the room and closet began to look like a hurricane had hit. Clothes were strewn everywhere — on the floor, on the furniture, on the bed, you name it. What a mess! Not to mention the time it took with this mess to decide on what to wear. Worse yet, once they identified one part of the outfit that they finally approved of, like pants, then the real anger and frustration became evident and you could hear, again and again: "Where the hell is the matching blouse?" as the search for the rest of the outfit continued.

Now imagine their added frustration when they discovered that the blouse they planned to wear was actually a little dirty or needed ironing. In addition, almost without failure, they would wind up racing the clock as they began to run late. By the time they were done, they had already become emotional wrecks. Is this the way to start a pleasant evening? Hardly!

Amazingly, no matter how many times we repeat the same cycle, we never seem to allow enough extra time to avoid this mad rush. So, here we are. We are, all of us, smart women who look forward to going out and spend time with friends, or enjoy a pleasant date. Instead, we end up with a major attack of anxiety in the process. Why don't we break this unnecessary, silly cycle? Why don't we enjoy the process of getting ready for a special occasion, making it as pleasant as the event itself? I can assure you that, if we did so, going out would become a much more enjoyable and memorable experience. This actually is very easy to do with just a little advanced planning and a well-organized closet.

Now that you are prepared to enjoy the whole process of getting ready, say for a lovely evening out, be sure to allow plenty of time to look in the mirror as much as you want and make any last minute minor adjustments to convince yourself that you look terrific. Not only will this create an optimal mood for you to welcome your date and enjoy the whole evening, but your demeanor will be more relaxed and you will be highly confident that you look great. When your confidence is higher, it radiates through your subconscious and you will appear at your best. You can bring this experience to the ultimate level if you also really love your clothes because they are comfortable, make you happy and you are convinced that they bring out the best in you. Can you see how everything works together in a closed circuit?

Love Your Clothes

Love your clothes and treat them well. That refers to all your clothes, not just the more expensive ones! You may ask, "What does it mean to treat your clothes well?" The answer is simple. If you take a look at how the more expensive stores display their clothes, you will notice that they are organized, neatly folded or hung, clean, displayed in a manner that is pleasing to the eyes, and are ready to wear. They appear to be just begging you to put them on and take them with you. Well, the clothes in your closet should look just as good and just as appealing and inviting. Only then will you more fully enjoy the process of getting ready. The psychology for you in this situation should be similar to being in a nice restaurant and experiencing the pleasure and built-up expectations as you see a beautiful presentation of food on your plate.

155

How to Organize Any Closet

You may wonder how you should go about organizing your closet. I understand that some of us are more fortunate than others and have large, walk-in closets, while others have very small closets. Clearly, it is easier to organize a larger closet, but, with some creativity and determination, a smaller one can be organized just as effectively. Currently, I am one of the very fortunate who has a large, walk-in closet. It is well-organized and the envy of many of my friends. However, this was not always the case. For many years I lived in a very small apartment with a "hole" in the wall as a closet. Yet, I can assure you that I was able to accomplish exactly the same organization even then.

Organization is just a function of determination, creativity, discipline and practice. For the purpose of this chapter, I will assume you have a larger closet. For those who have a smaller closet, I recommend that you use that closet for things that need to be hung. Anything that can be folded should be put into drawers or onto shelves. If you need more drawer space, you can use special containers that can fit under your bed or in other places.

Organizing a closet refers to two different things, how the closet appears physically and how you organize your belongings within that space. Many closets I've seen have their shelf and drawer space maximized instead of their hanging space. This arrangement may be appropriate for men, but does not work all that well for women. I believe that most of the built-in closets found in apartments and homes, whether they are the walk-in variety or not, were designed by male architects who have no concept of what women need. If you have an opportunity to design your own closet, keep this thought in mind — hanging space is preferable to drawers and shelf space.

If you can't change your closet, you need to do the best with what you currently have. Therefore, use the available hanging space to hang your more expensive garments and others in the following order: long formal dresses, other long dresses, skirts, jackets and light coats. If you have additional space, then hang your blouses, pants and jeans. If not enough space is available to accommodate everything, what can't be hung should be folded and kept neatly in drawers, on shelves or in special containers.

The most important item any closet should have is a full-length mirror. If possible, try to obtain a three-way mirror. It is worth both the trouble and the cost.

As far as actually organizing the clothes in your closet, here are two ways you may find helpful. One way is to organize by season, while the other is to organize by similar clothing categories, like by pants, jeans, dresses, skirts, jackets, etc.

I prefer to use the second method, which is to group similar categories of clothes and then group by color within each category.

To look more appealing, begin by hanging your long dresses at one end of the closet, followed by the knee-length and shorter dresses. Next, add your skirts followed by pants and jeans.

I hang my short coats, jackets and blouses in another section and use my shelves to place folded sweaters and my shoes. Nearly everything else belongs in drawers. Within each clothing section, I organize items by color, starting with the lighter ones first, followed by the stronger colors. This organization is not just eye-appealing, but will also allow you to find whatever you need very quickly.

To avoid the frustration of trying to decide what to wear, I always prepare my clothes the night before for the following day. I also select the outfit that I want to wear for a special event the night before I need to wear it. I do this not because I have time to waste, rather quite the opposite. I do this because experience has shown me that, overall, this is a more efficient way to prepare and avoid aggravation. After you are finished getting dressed up, don't forget to check your image in that full-length, three-way mirror. However, don't pose "Hollywood style" as you look at yourself, nor should you stand completely straight and stiff. Just stand naturally. Be relaxed and move a bit to check how you look in your most natural demeanor, as this is how the world will see you.

*T*welve Steps to a Clean, Organized Closet

A closet always should be clean. Below is what I periodically do to clean my closet; I recommend you do this with yours as well.

1. Remove everything from your closet — and I mean absolutely everything! This even includes those clothes and accessories you believe to be in a clean section, as well as those that are already so nicely arranged and folded you would hate to disturb. Take them all out, nothing should be left inside!

2. To clean the closet use your favorite cleaning agent that leaves behind a fresh and clean smell, and two cleaning cloths; one should be damp and the other dry. Systematically begin to clean every square inch of your closet to remove all dust and dirt. I mean, clean everything, including the walls, floor and shelving. Be very thorough, focusing on every nook and cranny, section by section; don't miss anything. Start with the walls, then do the shelves, and finish by cleaning the floor. When you wipe them clean, begin with the damp cloth and then follow immediately with the dry one. Don't be lazy! This is your treasure chest. You need to put a little elbow grease into this mission for it to accomplish your goal. Think of your closet as if it is an expensive store. It should be clean and smell nice.

3. Now you are ready to organize your clothes and return them to the closet. Before you do, take another look at what clothes you have and reassess whether you really need everything in your closet. Think about whether or not you really use all these clothes. If not, they should not be returned to the closet regardless of any wishful thinking you may have about using them one day. Now, I am not suggesting that you throw everything else away. If you think that you may wear them again in the future, like after you lose some weight, then it is fine not to throw them away. However, don't put them

back in your closet, either. Store them somewhere else until after you have lost the weight or are otherwise ready to wear them again. The rest you may consider just donating to charity.

Also, check to make sure that every item you do want to keep in the closet is clean, has all its buttons, doesn't require fixing and is otherwise absolutely ready to wear. If anything needs to be cleaned, ironed or fixed, then keep it out of your closet until after the appropriate repairs are completed.

4. Now we are finally ready to put all the remaining clothes back into the closet. To save space, use clip hangers for skirts and pants. To preserve the clothes better, use padded satin coat hangers for short coats, blouses, jackets and sweaters; and wide hangers for big coats. However, I suggest keeping most sweaters folded on shelves, if possible and you have the shelf space for it. This allows the sweaters to retain their shapes. You have probably noticed first-hand that when you hang sweaters, they tend to stretch out over time and lose their shape due to gravity. Also, if possible, do not hang multiple items on a single hanger, as the whole idea of a good organization is to have the ability to quickly scan what you have so you can best decide what to wear. With multiple items on a single hanger, that would be very difficult to do.

163

5. You are now ready to hang your clothes. Decide whether you prefer to organize your clothing by category or by season. I recommend that you organize by category. Within each category, you should organize by season, and within each season organize by color. Please note that when you hang your long dresses, try to hang them so they do not touch the floor. If this is impossible, take the lower part of the dress and fold it over the top of the hanger.

6. **Shoes** I find, more often than not, that shoes are the most neglected items in our closets. Many of us do not worry about them much since they are so small and are worn at the absolutely lowest part of our body, making them less noticeable and therefore less worthy of special attention. This is wrong! Don't act like the clueless men who put on a fancy suit, but wear shoes badly in need of a shoeshine, or with heels that badly need fixing. Remember how quickly you notice these kinds of things and what you think of this kind of man? Take care not to fall into that same trap!

Before you organize your shoes, make sure they are clean and are not in need of repair. Otherwise, you should clean them and take them to a shoe repair shop if they are worth fixing. I also recommend that you get in the habit of stuffing any closed shoes and boots with papers, special shoetrees or other shape protectors to help them keep their shapes. By the way, some women keep their shoes in the original boxes they came with at purchase. I do not recommend doing so. First, these boxes take a lot of space and, secondly, it is unlikely you will remember which shoes are inside. Therefore, put your shoes on any available shelves. If you don't have shelves, just put them on the floor below the hanging clothes. This way you can spot them quickly. As a personal note, I also organize my shoes by season, followed by color.

I keep my boots, sneakers, flip-flops, etc., in a place separate from my dressy shoes. My sandals are on the top shelf, followed by my low-heeled and open shoes, as well as my lower-heeled closed shoes. On the lowest shelf are my low-heeled ankle and other boots. In other words, put all your lighter weight shoes on the upper shelves and the heavier ones on the bottom. Should you need more space, plastic pockets and shoe-holders that hang on the back of your closet door can be used.

7. **Bags** I love bags! In an ideal world, you should store your bags in an open space where you can see them. If you have the luxury of this extra open space, store them on the shelves of your closet for easy access. Unfortunately, I don't have that extra space, so I keep my bags inside drawers and closed cabinets. If you have no extra drawer or cabinet space then another good way to store your bags is in a big plastic storage container.

8. **Undergarments** I am pretty sure everyone has special drawers. To save time when looking for them, I recommend separating your bras, underwear, tights, pantyhose and socks. Using dividers or containers that fit in the drawer to separate the items will make it an easier task.

9. **Hats** Hats can be interesting when it comes to storage. They can be stacked up or placed on shelves, like I store them. However, if you have the space and you do not own too many hats, you may want to hang them on hooks, which will preserve their shape better.

10. **Winter coats** Winter coats should not be neglected. Use wide, wooden hangers for heavy coats. I keep my heavy winter coats in a separate closet stored inside special bags so they don't collect dust. By the way, you should never store coats in plastic covers since coats need to breathe. This is particularly true of fur coats. Fur coats must be stored properly to maintain a fresh look. If you can afford it, have your more expensive fur coats stored at a special fur storage facility, found at almost any fur store.

11. Belts In my closet, I have a section with special hooks where I hang my belts so I can see all of them at a glance. I know that many women have a special box in which they store their belts, which is fine as well.

12. **Scarves** These accessories introduce a bit of a dilemma as they are not the easiest to store. Ideally, like belts, scarves could hang on hooks; alternatively, they can be folded and placed on shelves as the next best storage remedy. Either way, you can easily see all of them at the same time, which will help make decisions about which one to wear much easier.

Now that you are done organizing your closet, review and enjoy it — and enjoy it you will! I understand that going through all the cleaning and reorganization can be painful and dreadful to think about, but, trust me. When all is done, you will feel great and enjoy looking at the results of your labor. More importantly, you will be able to really enjoy the process of dressing up and getting ready for a special event.

Chapter 11

> "WHEN I SEE PEOPLE DRESSED IN HIDEOUS CLOTHES THAT LOOK ALL WRONG ON THEM, I TRY TO IMAGINE THE MOMENT WHEN THEY WERE BUYING THEM AND THOUGHT 'THIS IS GREAT. I LIKE IT. I'LL TAKE IT'."
>
> · · · · · ANDY WARHOL · · ·

SHOPPING FOR CLOTHES

By now you understand the difference between fashion and style. However, more importantly, you understand the importance of PERSONAL STYLE! You understand your body type and the clothes that work best for you, as well as which colors work for you and which don't. Now, we are ready to go shopping!

Shopping is not a chore for most women, even though it tends to be for men. We women don't just walk into a store to purchase something that seems functional enough for what we want, and then exit just as quickly as we entered. Instead, for us, shopping is an experience! We prefer to take our time. We like to explore what is new and different, try things on and kill time looking around as many stores as time allows. To top it all off, we absolutely just love to have our friends join us to catch up on gossip.

In other words, shopping is not a chore for us, but an enjoyable pastime. It also is amazing to see how shopping transforms instantaneously from merely being an enjoyable activity into an exciting experience filled with elation when we actually end up buying something. Boy, it does make us feel so good! I truly believe the often heard cliché that shopping is actually a therapeutic experience for

171

most women, and may even be cheaper than going to a psychologist when we need to feel better! Well, on second thought, maybe not really that cheaper. However, we surely can take steps to at least make shopping less costly for us (or our husbands).

Unfortunately, as many of us have learned the hard way, shopping can be very expensive and, worse yet, wasteful! Most of us don't mind spending money on nice clothes when we love them — even if we max out our credit cards. However, we don't much like the way we feel when, subsequently, we realize that we bought something expensive that we find we no longer love and seldom, if ever, will wear. As odd as this may sound, we all fall into the same trap over and over again. Wouldn't it be better if we could only become a little smarter and avoid this from occurring in the first place?

I love shopping and all aspects of the shopping experience. Trust me. I have made my share of mistakes and have suffered my share of subsequent regrets. Now that I've become much wiser about style and shopping, I consider myself a more sophisticated shopper.

Please allow me to share with you some rules that, hopefully, will enhance your shopping experience, minimize your regrets and save you money in the process. They also provide you with even more reasons to make you feel less guilty about spending money to buy this book!

Below is a set of rules I recommend to help you with your shopping experience. Please don't view these rules, with the typical cliché that we American view rules — rules are meant to be broken! Instead, please read them carefully, try to follow them and allow yourself to enjoy the results.

The Magic of Style by Larisa Kronfeld

The 16 Essential Rules for Clothes Shopping

*R*ule 1 - There is nothing wrong with **shopping**. It is the **buying** that may lead us astray. Remember that shopping is actually an enjoyable activity and so you may enjoy it as often as time allows and as long as you are in the mood.

*R*ule 2 - There is nothing wrong with **buying**; however, it's when you **buy the wrong items** that the activity becomes wasteful and regrettable. As I mentioned earlier, the act of buying actually can create an elating experience. It is only after some time passes that we may regret a purchase that we no longer like. Therefore, the obvious, logical conclusion is to buy as much as you like and can afford. But, don't fall prey and buy something that you later may not like or use.

*R*ule 3 - Avoid "spur of the moment" or impulsive purchases and never buy clothes when you are in a hurry. Rationalize and identify in advance exactly what you would like to buy and why. As examples, you might decide, "I need to buy a long, lightweight autumn coat because I don't have one;" or "I need to buy an upscale jacket for special evenings at nice places because I don't have one and I could use one;" or "I need a knee-length dress for work."

Once you know what you want to buy and why, then conceptualize in advance exactly what you are looking for in terms of length, style, cut, color, etc. Use all the logic and resources that this book has provided.

Now, go shopping any time you want, but only purchase what you have identified in advance. Never buy anything different that may appeal to you on impulse. Never break this rule by rationalizing why, this time, it is a worthwhile exception. If you succumb, you are much more likely to regret it! However, if you can't help it and have rationalized an exception because you feel very strongly that this time you are sure that you know what you are doing, then my advice is to not make the purchase at that time, but wait a day or two. Then return to the store to see if you still feel the same way and want to buy it just as badly as the first time.

*R*ule 4 - Never buy any clothes, particularly designer clothes just because they are on sale and you can get them at a great price. How many times have I heard about a woman who bought designer label clothes because they were marked at a bargain price? I have to admit that I have fallen into this trap myself. As I have reiterated many times throughout this book, there is a difference between fashion and style and a difference between clothes that make you look great and clothes that don't. Remember, a designer label does not guarantee a look that is complimentary to you!

$\mathcal{R}$ule 5 - Never buy "fashion," but, instead, always follow your personal style! You need to feel comfortable in your clothes and should purchase only those that go well with your personal style, as described in this book. In fact, it is best if you just **l-o-o-o-o-v-e** what you are about to buy and feel as if it was made especially for you.

$\mathcal{R}$ule 6 - Strive to buy clothes that have multiple uses and are multi-purpose. This means, clothes that you can wear for more than one occasion and better yet, clothes that you can combine with other items to create a variety of outfits for different occasions. So, for example, avoid buying a blouse which only matches one suit. Look for the blouse that you can wear with a minimum of three outfits that you already own.

$\mathcal{R}$ule 7 - Unless you are loaded with money and can afford to waste it, don't buy any clothes that are in fashion for only one season. As I have emphasized throughout the book, strive to buy the kinds of clothes that never lose their charm and will always be in style. View your clothes as an important "collection" of carefully selected, well-fitting, beautiful items you love and enjoy and have collected over a long period of time.

*R*ule 8 - Never buy something which is not your size, or doesn't fit perfectly. Understand that larger-sized clothes tend to make a woman look older, while smaller-sized ones make a woman look fatter. Also, smaller, really tight clothing make a woman look tactless and completely undermine any hint of femininity.

At the same time, no matter how much you really like a garment or its great bargain price, if it doesn't fit you perfectly, move on. Be careful about buying clothes that don't fit well and will require subsequent alterations to make them fit better. If you decide to purchase them, you should have real understanding of tailoring and be certain that the required modifications can be made properly. Oftentimes, alterations destroy the original "lines" and what was beautiful becomes distorted. These distortions may be subtle but at times quite apparent. Worse yet, many tailors who don't charge outrageous rates are not all that great in the first place and their work leaves much to be desired. I always have been amazed at how women notice all these imperfections and distorted fits on other women, particularly on women they don't like or are envious of, but rarely seem to observe the same imperfections on themselves. This rule is also true even for in-store alterations, unless the store is very high-end and you know and have a great deal of confidence in their tailor. Not included in this rule, of course, are simple conventional tailoring adjustments like those to add a hem, shorten a length, shorten straps, etc.

Rule 9 - Never regret not making a purchase. Trust me, you'll always find something even more beautiful in the future!

$\mathcal{R}$ule 10 - Buy good quality clothes that will last. Cheaply made clothes rarely last, meaning you will end up spending more money to replenish them. Now, don't jump to the conclusion that I advocate buying expensive or designer clothes. On the contrary! Although expensive designer clothes generally are of higher quality and most likely will last longer, it is not necessarily true in all cases. More importantly, a large selection of clothes is available that may not be the cheapest, but also are not very expensive, yet offer excellent quality for a very reasonable price.

$\mathcal{R}$ule 11 - Be a patient buyer! Never buy anything toward the end of a long shopping day just because you are disappointed at not finding something to buy. Yes, making a "desperation purchase" may make you feel better and give you a sense that the day was "productive" because you actually bought something, but, more likely, the feeling will be short-lived and you'll end up regretting it.

$\mathcal{R}$ule 12 - Never purchase or wear anything that is an obvious copy of expensive designer clothes, or accessories. Everyone will likely know that it is a knock-off, as they have probably seen it everywhere, and the more discerning buyers can tell anyways, and you will appear "cheap" and pretentious.

$\mathcal{R}$ule 13 - The best buys are clothes that you purchase on sale! Now, please note that I am not at all suggesting that you should feel comfortable taking advantage of a great sale and buy some clothes. Instead I am saying that once you decided to buy something, then wait to buy it when it goes on sale with a marked down price. Remember, throughout this book I've recommended that you buy clothes that will remain in style and usable for years. Therefore, there is no need to buy them at the height of a season and at their highest prices.

$\mathcal{R}$ule 14 - You can make an exception to the rules cited above from time to time if you really, really love something, even if you haven't identified the item in advance or really need it, as long as it promises to provide multiple uses over many years. It becomes even more permissible if it is unique, not a typical item that sells anywhere else including in department stores and designer chain stores.

$\mathcal{R}$ule 15 - Never, **ever** listen to a sales person when you decide to buy. First of all, most have no concept of what really looks good or fits your personal style well — unless, of course, they read this book and tell you so. Secondly, most really don't care much about you. Instead, they are working to make a living and will try their best to convince you to buy anything.

Be assured, also, that most salespeople are not on salary and will try and convince you to buy items on which they make the most commissions. Don't be fooled!

$\mathcal{R}$ule 16 - If you truly like something that is too expensive for your budget but you decided to buy it regardless, then remind yourself you can very possibly find something quite **similar** for less money, perhaps in another brand or store. Only if you really believe that to be impossible should you go ahead and buy it. However, make sure that you are really, really honest with yourself and not just being lazy, trying to avoid looking around for something similar when this piece is right in front of you, begging you to take it home.

Chapter 12

ATTITUDE, BEHAVIOR AND STYLE

Many women believe that being attractive, stylish, fashionable, feminine, sexy, or whichever other adjective might be used in this context, is a function of three things:

- How naturally physically attractive they are based on the attributes they were born with;

- How they groom themselves, which would include hairstyles and makeup;

- The clothes they wear.

While these three elements are true, they miss an essential factor, one that I believe is actually very important. Most of us don't consciously think of it, but subconsciously do react to it. This factor concerns our **attitudes and behavior!**

I am sure that you have had ample opportunities to experience firsthand how someone's attitude and behavior affected whether you found them more or less attractive, but may not have really connected all the dots and noticed them in yourself. So, please allow me to make some observations to help your awareness, so that you could use it to your advantage. However, what I am going to tell you is more applicable to the reaction you can expect from men; women may or may not react the same way.

You may ask, why am I bringing up to your attentions how men react, while I know that we mostly dress to catch the attention of other women, and that men rarely observe the level of details that women naturally do.

The answer is simple. While primarily, we try to impress other women, we also greatly want to appear attractive to men. In fact, if a woman is single, attracting a man often becomes a top priority. That is until we catch our man and can again re-shift our attention to making other women envious

183

of our clothes and looks. There is another important reason, besides a romantic relationship, to appear attractive to men. As I mentioned earlier in the book, everyone — men and women alike — are dependent on those around us in almost every aspect of our lives. Men, much more so than women, become more helpful to women they find attractive and appealing. Although men are not as observant to details involved in fashion and style, they do react to the overall looks, and do react to some behavioral traits. Therefore, becoming aware of those behavioral traits men react to and using them to our advantage is definitely of value.

You may not agree at first with some of my comments regarding men's reactions, because they may contradict your own experience with how your male friends react and what they tell you. However, please don't dismiss my observations. My observations apply more to men who are not already good friends of yours. Those who are friends have adjusted their subconscious reactions and view you as a "friend" rather than as a "woman." The same is true about family members. How you behave around them and how they react to you is different from how other men and in other circumstances will react.

One additional point: after reading my observations you may discover some "bad" behavioral traits within yourself and believe that they are uncorrectable, because they have been part of you forever. Please don't become discouraged. The behavioral attributes that I will identify are completely within your power to control and change over time, but your awareness, as the first step, is paramount.

$\mathcal{N}$ine Observations about Attitudes and Behavior

Observation 1 - A smiling face ALWAYS makes a woman look more attractive and appealing.

Observation 2 - Shy and polite behavior ALWAYS makes a woman look more attractive and appealing.

Observation 3 - Casual flirting ALWAYS makes a woman more appealing, however, be careful with this one, as you don't want to alienate a man's wife or girlfriend.

Observation 4 - An angry face NEVER looks attractive or appealing.

Observation 5 - Loud voices and loud laughter DETRACT from FEMININITY. By "loud" I don't mean using a raised voice when you are angry — although this observation will definitely apply to this situation as well. I refer to a naturally occurring loud voice, the kind that can be heard at the next table in a restaurant, or one that "carries" across a room. The reaction is even worse when a voice is not only loud in volume, but also has a higher pitch. Since I included loud laughter in this observation your first reaction may well be, "What are you talking about? My friends (or I) love the person with loud laughter, it is so catchy!" While this may be true, please remember, as mentioned earlier, friends, family members and those who are not reacting to you as a woman may love it, but, believe me, for anyone else, these vocal elements will detract from your femininity. Also, avoid speaking in normal volume in enclosed spaces, like elevators, small rooms, restaurants, etc.

$\mathcal{O}$bservation 6 - A negative attitude is rarely attractive or appealing. Here attitude refers to your personality. Are you naturally optimistic or pessimistic? Are you self-confident or do you have a "defeatist" attitude? Do you always see problems or obstacles when it comes to things and plans, or are your opinions balanced? Do you criticize more than you compliment? Do you see a glass half full, or half empty?

$\mathcal{O}$bservation 7 - Personalities that frequently complain, nag, whine or are angry NEVER look attractive or appealing. Here I am referring to a pattern of behavior and not to single occurrences. Of course, I know that we women sometimes have to "nag" to get a man to do what we want. Otherwise, we are likely to get nothing post the initial courting phase, when we got so much without even asking. In other words, "nagging" for a woman to some extent is a necessity. However, avoid doing so when you are in the very early stages of a relationship. Later on, if you must resort to nagging to get your way or have him do what you want, then do it in the "right" way. Many of us learned the "right" way as little girls when we wanted something from our fathers that Mom had probably refused already — we asked in a "cutesy" way. So, when you need to "nag," do it in a little girl's way with a cute expression that makes it appear as if you are being "playful" — men always fall for that! (Gee, I hope your boyfriends or husbands will never read this page!)

Observation 8 - The use of curse words NEVER comes across attractively, not even when used in a joking, light hearted manner. In particularly, avoid using the "F" word, which nowadays appears to be prevalent and therefore perhaps more acceptable. Don't be fooled. It is never appropriate for a woman to use words like this. Of course, it's not as bad if you are among good friends, but it is best to avoid it if you can.

Observation 9 - Drunken behavior is, more often than not, unattractive. As we all know, alcohol and over-drinking affects different people differently. There is no clear and fast rule about "drunken" behavior. If becoming tipsy quiets you, or makes you become more smiley or a bit flirtier, then it is not that bad. In fact, many men may find women who are tipsy in such a manner somewhat cute and attractive. However, if you are a person who becomes louder, more aggressive, more confrontational, more argumentative, less coherent or tend to use curse words, you are not likely to be appealing. In fact, most likely you will be perceived as being unfeminine and crude! Certainly avoid, at all costs, drinking to the point where you begin to lose your balance or begin to stumble when you walk or talk.

I hope I have convinced you that our behavior is important and if you lack in any particular trait then you should try to change it. I know that changing ones behavior is easier said than done, but there is no substitute to trying. All you need to do is to try your best, it may be slow at first and appear uncomfortable, but persevere and over time it will get easier and easier to a point where it will finally become second nature and permanent.

Conclusions

> "ART PRODUCES UGLY THINGS WHICH FREQUENTLY BECOME BEAUTIFUL WITH TIME. FASHION, ON THE OTHER HAND, PRODUCES BEAUTIFUL THINGS WHICH BECOME UGLY WITH TIME."
> ····· JEAN COTEAU ···

Congratulations! You have made it through this book and I hope you enjoyed reading it as much as I enjoyed writing it. By now you should have a greater understanding of what personal style is and how not to confuse it with fashion. You now know what to look for and what to avoid. You have a better understanding of how to emphasize your natural gifts and how to mask the parts you don't like all that much. Best of all, you now know what to look for when you observe other women and how they dress. I'll bet that when you apply the principles found in this book to observe other women, you will find yourself laughing at times. Laughter is good for your health. (This is yet another reason not to regret the expense of purchasing this book, as spending money beneficial to your health should never be an expense to regret!)

Seriously, after reading this book, you know a lot. However, you learned merely the theory so you are only book smart. As with any other theory, you need experience to effectively put it to use. As this book suggests, experience comes from practice — from constant looking, observing, experimenting and evaluating. I assure you that, after a while, it will become second nature and you will officially become a style maven.

I'd like to offer one last piece of advice, which was mentioned in the book but not emphasized much, as I wanted to hold it until the end. This book mostly discussed how you can look more **attractive and appealing**. Included were some behavioral traits that may make you more or less attractive. I have one additional observation, which is, perhaps, the most important of them all and affects how attractive you appear to others. **You are as attractive as you believe you are!**

I know — like motherhood and apple pie — it sounds clichéd. Indeed it is, but there is substance to it as well. There are a vast number of women, and you may be one of them, who do not believe they are attractive. The odd thing is that, even naturally attractive women suffer this same lack of confidence because they see things in themselves they don't like. There is value in overcoming such a perception, as it affects their behavior and how attractively they come across to other people. To help you overcome this, I would like to point out two things.

First, we all tend to be our own worst critics. More often than not, we see things about our bodies that no one else even notices. This is simple to understand. When we look at ourselves, we focus on every square inch of our bodies and use our eyes as if they were microscopes. On the other hand, when others look at us, they take in the full picture and most details are not noticed.

Just compare how we look at hairdos. We labor over every little hair to make sure it is not out of place, and God knows, we see them all, yet anyone else looking at us sees the whole hairdo and will rarely, if ever, notice that one piece of hair may be misplaced. Ask yourself if, indeed, there is a difference between how you look and judge yourself and how you look and judge others. What does it all mean? It means, that whatever you believe to be unattractive about yourself is most likely not as noticeable by others. In other words, others view you to be more attractive than you view yourself. This is true; believe it!

Second, we all understand that clothing, a hairdo and makeup strongly affect how attractive we appear to others. After all, we spend zillions of dollars every year on these items just for that very reason. Even if you are not fully convinced of the observation in the previous paragraph, at least accept that you can mask it with your clothes, hairdo and makeup, and appear much more attractive than you think you really are. So, apply what you learned from this book and believe that as a result you indeed look your best.

Now, here is the "kicker:" The more you believe that you look your best, the more attractive you'll be perceived. In other words, your behavior, personality and disposition are subconsciously affected by how comfortable and confident you are. As humans, we are "wired" to perceive and react to such subtle signals at the subconscious level. At the same time, we also tend to find people who project comfort and confidence to be more attractive to us. Therefore, if you believe that you are attractive, then your entire body language will react accordingly and exude comfort and confidence in a way that actually make you appear more attractive to other people, and vice versa. Now you understand why I stress, "You are as attractive as you believe you are!"

Practice and follow what you learned in this book: (a) use the right clothes; (b) adopt appropriate behaviors; (c) feel confident and, viola — you will be attractive and there will be no one else like you. You now will be uniquely attractive in your own way. Be confident that you are special because there are no two people who are alike, who combine these three elements the same way. You are indeed special — and it is that combination that makes you powerful and more attractive. More importantly, men always react to the combination of these three things; so, if you feel you lack one, make up for it with the others!

The only other thing left is to remind you that to be stylish and attractive does not require having a lot of money. All you need is discipline, experience and balance.

I hope that you will develop your personal style and, one day, will walk down the street and hear the greatest possible compliment — another woman saying, "I want to look like you!" — or, at least, "Wow! You look wonderful!" or hear a man saying, "You look great!"

I would love to hear from you. Please visit my website, www.themagicofstyle.com and share your comments and thoughts.

Enjoy shopping!